UNSPEAKABLE
VERSE

UNSPEAKABLE

❖

VERSE

As read on BBC by Miriam Margolyes, Leo
McKern, Hugh Laurie and Louise Lombard

Anthology by Patricia Houlihan

GRIFFIN PRODUCTIONS

B❖XTREE

First published in the UK in 1996 by Boxtree Limited,
Broadwall House, 21 Broadwall, London, SE1 9PL

ISBN: 0 7522 0239 1

10 9 8 7 6 5 4 3 2 1

Printed and bound in Great Britain by The Bath Press, Somerset

A CIP catalogue entry for this book is available from the
British Library

Cassette available from Reed Audio

CONTENTS

THE LION AND ALBERT
George Marriott Edgar

LORD FINCHLEY
Hilaire Belloc
PRELUDE
Wendy Cope
I'VE BEEN TO A MARVELLOUS PARTY
Noël Coward
LIMERICK
Anon
THE SONG OF THE QUOODLE
G. K. Chesterton
SYMPTOM RECITAL
Dorothy Parker
A WORD OF ENCOURAGEMENT
J. R. Pope
MUNGOJERRIE AND RUMPELTEAZER
T. S. Eliot
AUTUMN
Stevie Smith
ALWAYS TRUE TO YOU IN MY FASHION
Cole Porter
REBECCA WHO SLAMMED DOORS FOR FUN AND
PERISHED MISERABLY
Hilaire Belloc
AS I WAS GOING UP THE STAIR
Anon
FATIGUE
Hilaire Belloc

PIG RHYME
Jan Morris
WHEN YOU ARE OLD AND GREY
Tom Lehrer
LOVEY-DOVEY
Anon

FOREWORD

If you already have a passion for poetry, feel free to skip this bit, but if not, just give me a moment. This is bold of me, for the greatest poets have tried – and sometimes failed – to explain why poetry is both wondrous and important. The danger is that you can sound awfully pompous. However, I happen to know that people *loved* our television series 'Unspeakable Verse' and that's because so many of you wrote and told me so (something which is almost unheard of in the wonderful world of television). You 'sat and chuckled and hugged yourselves with delight.' So I'm not at all worried about you.

However, I am concerned about those people – sadly, mostly young people – who *would* love it, but just will never know. They've never been given the chance to love it. Our programmes were an attempt to let those people know that poetry is there for them. It is a huge treasure-house of language that they can go and play in, and then they too will end up hugging themselves with delight.

'Unspeakable Verse' shows that poetry can make you laugh, and once it has done that, well then you may find it can make you cry as well. Only then can you begin to understand that it's there to show that you're part of an enormous, overwhelming, age-old nexus of human emotion and intellect. You need never feel that you're out there on your own again, because it's all there just for you.

Hopefully, we'll be doing some more programmes mining the great and astoundingly rich seam of British verse; but in the meantime, you must rush out and buy *lots* of copies of this anthology and immediately give them to anyone you feel just might have poetry in their soul, particularly anyone under thirty who might not know it yet. If this sounds vulgar, you should know that this testimonial is completely untainted by commercial considerations. For me, this is a labour of deepest and abiding love. So, as they say, let me share it with you!

Patricia Houlihan
Producer and Director of 'Unspeakable Verse'

LIST OF READERS

Initials are given after each poem title.

Hugh Laurie (**HL**)
Louise Lombard (**LL**)
Leo McKern (**LM**)
Miriam Margolyes (**MM**)

Programme 1

INDIFFERENCE
Harry Graham (LM)

When Grandmamma fell off the boat,
And couldn't swim (and wouldn't float)
Matilda just stood by and smiled
I almost could have slapped the child

JIM WHO RAN AWAY FROM HIS NURSE AND WAS EATEN BY A LION
Hilaire Belloc (MM)

There was a Boy whose name was Jim;
His Friends were very good to him.
They gave him Tea, and Cakes, and Jam,
And slices of delicious Ham,
And Chocolate with pink inside,
And little Tricycles to ride,
And read him Stories through and through,
And even took him to the Zoo—
But there it was the dreadful Fate
Befell him, which I now relate.

You know – at least you ought to know,
For I have often told you so –
That Children never are allowed
To leave their Nurses in a Crowd;
Now this was Jim's especial Foible,
He ran away when he was able,
And on this inauspicious day
He slipped his hand and ran away!
He hadn't gone a yard when – Bang!
With open Jaws, a Lion sprang,
And hungrily began to eat
The Boy: beginning at his feet.

Now, just imagine how it feels
When first your toes and then your heels,
And then by gradual degrees,
Your shins and ankles, calves and knees,
Are slowly eaten, bit by bit.
No wonder Jim detested it!
No wonder that he shouted 'Hi'!
The Honest Keeper heard his cry,
Though very fat he almost ran
To help the little gentleman.
'Ponto!' he ordered as he came
(For Ponto was the Lion's name),
'Ponto!' he cried, with angry Frown.
'Let go, Sir! Down, Sir! Put it down!'

The Lion made a sudden Stop,
He let the Dainty Morsel drop,
And slunk reluctant to his Cage,
Snarling with Disappointed Rage.
But when he bent over Jim,
The Honest Keeper's Eyes were dim.
The Lion having reached his Head,
The Miserable Boy was dead!
When Nurse informed his Parents, they
Were more Concerned than I can say:-
His Mother, as she dried her eyes,
Said, 'Well – it gives me no surprise,
He would not do as he was told!'
His Father, who was self-controlled,
Bade all the children round attend
To James' miserable end,
And always keep a-hold of Nurse
For fear of finding something worse.

LOSS
Wendy Cope (LL)

The day he moved out was terrible
That evening she went through hell
His absence wasn't a problem
But the corkscrew was gone as well.

I'M THE DOG WHO DIDN'T WIN A PRIZE
Pam Ayres (HL)

I'm the dog who didn't win a prize
I didn't have the Most Appealing Eyes.
All day in this heat, I've been standing on my feet
With dogs of every other shape and size.

I've been harshly disinfected, I've been snubbed
I've been festooned in a towel and I've been rubbed
I've been mercilessly brushed, robbed of all my fleas and dust
And now the judging's over: I've been snubbed.

Was it for obedience I was hailed?
As 'Best Dog in the Show' was I regaled?
O not on your Doggo life, pass me down the carving knife,
I had one thing said about me – it was 'FAILED'.

I never for a moment thought I'd fail
I thought at least I'd win 'Waggiest Tail'
But no certificate, rosette or commendation did I get –
Nothing on the kennel door to nail.

I am going in my kennel on my own
Thank you no, I do not want a bone.
Do not think you can console me with left-overs in my bowl
My pride is mortified – I want to be alone.

I've heard it from the worldly and the wise:
'Each dog has his day' they all advise,
But I see to my grief and sorrow,
My day must have been tomorrow!
Oh I'm the dog who didn't win a prize!

SLOUGH
John Betjeman (LM)

Come friendly bombs, and fall on Slough
It isn't fit for humans now,
There isn't grass to graze a cow
Swarm over, Death!

Come, bombs, and blow to smithereens
Those air-conditioned, bright canteens,
Tinned fruit, tinned meat, tinned milk, tinned beans,
Tinned minds, tinned breath.

Mess up the mess they call a town —
A house for ninety-seven down
And once a week a half-a-crown
For twenty years,

And get that man with double chin
Who'll always cheat and always win,
Who washes his repulsive skin
In women's tears,

And smash his desk of polished oak
And smash his hands so used to stroke
And stop his boring dirty joke
And make him yell.

But spare the bald young clerks who add
The profits of the stinking cad;
It's not their fault that they are mad,
They've tasted Hell.

It's not their fault they do not know
The birdsong from the radio,
It's not their fault they often go
To Maidenhead

And talk of sports and makes of cars
In various bogus Tudor bars
And daren't look up and see the stars
But belch instead.

In labour-saving homes, with care
Their wives frizz out peroxide hair
And dry it in synthetic air
And paint their nails.

Come, friendly bombs, and fall on Slough
To get it ready for the plough.
The cabbages are coming now;
The earth exhales.

THE MOCK TURTLE'S SONG
Lewis Carroll (LM)

'Will you walk a little faster?' said a whiting to a snail.
'There's a porpoise close behind us, and he's treading on my
    tail.
See how eagerly the lobsters and the turtles all advance!
They are waiting on the shingle – will you come and join the
    dance?
Will you, won't you, will you, won't you, will you join the
    dance?
Will you, won't you, will you, won't you, won't you join
    the dance?

'You can really have no notion how delightful it will be,
When they take us up and throw us, with the lobsters, out to
    sea!'
But the snail replied 'Too far, too far!' and gave a look
    askance –
Said he thanked the whiting kindly, but he would not join
    the dance.
Would not, could not, would not, could not, would not join
    the dance.
Would not, could not, would not, could not, could not join
    the dance.

'What matters it how far we go?' his scaly friend replied.
'There is another shore, you know, upon the other side.
The further off from England the nearer is to France –
Then turn not pale, beloved snail, but come and join the
    dance.
Will you, won't you, will you, won't you, will you join the
    dance?
Will you, won't you, will you, won't you, won't you join
    the dance?

LOVE CONQUERS
Spike Milligan (MM)

As I watched her walk
Across the Heath,
Black was the colour
Of my true love's teeth.

As I watched him wander
Through the fair,
Bald was the colour
Of my true love's hair.

A LITTLE NUT-TREE
Roald Dahl (HL)

I had a little nut-tree,
Nothing would it bear.
I searched in all its branches,
But not a nut was there.

'Oh little tree,' I begged,
'Give me just a few.'
The little tree looked down at me
And whispered, 'Nuts to you.'

A BAR ON THE PICCOLA MARINA
by Noël Coward (MM)

In a 'bijou' abode
In St Barnabas Road
Not far from the Esher by-pass
Lived a mother and wife
Who, most of her life,
Let every adventure fly past.
She had two strapping daughters and a rather dull son
And a much duller husband who at sixty-one
Elected to retire
And, later on, expire,
Sing Hallelujah, Hey nonny-no, Hey nonny-no, Hey
    nonny-no!
He joined the feathered choir.
On a wet afternoon
In the middle of June
They all of them came home soaking
Having laid him to rest
By special request
In the family vault at Woking,
And then in the middle of the funeral wake
With her mouth full of excellent Madeira cake
His widow cried, 'That's done,
My life's at last begun,
Sing Hallelujah, Hey nonny-no, Hey nonny-no, Hey
    nonny-no,
It's time I had some fun,
Today, though hardly a jolly day,
At least has set me free,
We'll all have a lovely holiday
On the island of Capri!'

In a bar on the Piccola Marina
Life called to Mrs Wentworth-Brewster,
Fate beckoned her and introduced her
Into a rather queer
Unfamiliar atmosphere.
She'd just sit there, propping up the bar
Beside a fisherman who sang to a guitar.
When accused of having gone too far

8

She merely cried, 'Funiculi!
Just fancy me!
Funicula!'
When he bellowed 'Che Bella Signorina!'
Sheer ecstasy at once produced a
Wild shriek from Mrs Wentworth-Brewster,
Changing her whole demeanour.
When both her daughters and her son said,
'Please come home, Mama,'
She murmured rather bibulously, 'Who do you think you
    are?'
Nobody can afford to be so lahdy-bloody-da
In a bar on the Piccola Marina.

Every fisherman cried,
'Viva Viva' and 'Che Ragazza',
When she sat in the Grand Piazza
Everybody would rise,
Every fisherman sighed,
'Viva Viva che bell' Inglesi',
Someone even said, 'Whoops-a-daisy!'
Which was quite a surprise.
Each night she'd make some gay excuse
And beaming with good will
She'd just slip into something loose
And totter down the hill.

To the bar on the Piccola Marina
Where love came to Mrs Wentworth-Brewster,
Hot flushes of delight suffused her,
Right round the bend she went,
Picture her astonishment,
Day in, day out she would gad about
Because she felt she was no longer on the shelf,
Night out, night in, knocking back the gin
She'd cry, 'Hurrah!
Funicula
Funiculi
Funic yourself!'
Just for fun three young sailors from Messina
Bowed low to Mrs Wentworth-Brewster,
Said 'Scusi' and politely goosed her.

And then there was quite a scena.
Her family, in floods of tears, cried,
'Leave these men, Mama.'
She said, 'They're just high-spirited, like all Italians are
And most of them have a great deal more to offer than Papa
In a bar on the Piccola Marina.'

Programme 2

EXECUTIVE
John Betjeman (HL)

I am a young executive. No cuffs than mine are cleaner;
I have a Slimline brief-case and I use the firm's Cortina.
In every roadside hostelry from here to Burgess Hill
The *maîtres d'hôtel* all know me well and let me sign the bill.

You ask me what it is I do. Well actually, you know,
I'm partly a liaison man and partly P.R.O.
Essentially I integrate the current export drive
And basically I'm viable from ten o'clock till five.

For vital off-the-record work – that's talking transport wise –
I've a scarlet Aston-Martin – and does she go? She flies!
Pedestrians and dogs and cats – we mark them down for
    slaughter.
I also own a speed-boat which has never touched the water.

She's built of fibre-glass, of course. I call her 'Mandy Jane'
After a bird I used to know – No soda, please, just plain –
And how did I acquire her? Well to tell you about that
And to put you in the picture I must wear my other hat.

I do some mild developing. The sort of place I need
Is a quiet country market town that's rather run to seed.
A luncheon and a drink or two, a little *savoir faire* –
I fix the Planning Officer, the Town Clerk and the Mayor.

And if some preservationist attempts to interfere
A 'dangerous structure' notice from the Borough Engineer
Will settle any buildings that are standing in our way –
The modern style, sir, with respect, has really come to stay.

MRS WORTHINGTON
Noël Coward (MM)

Regarding yours, dear Mrs Worthington,
of Wednesday the 23rd,
Although your baby
May be
Keen on a stage career,
How can I make it clear,
That this is not a good idea.
For her to hope,
Dear Mrs Worthington,
Is on the face of it absurd,
Her personality
Is not in reality
Inviting enough,
Exciting enough
For this particular sphere.

Don't put your daughter on the stage, Mrs Worthington,
Don't put your daughter on the stage,
The profession is overcrowded
And the struggle's pretty tough
And admitting the fact
She's burning to act,
That isn't quite enough.
She has nice hands, to give the wretched girl her due,
But don't you think her bust is too
Developed for her age,
I repeat,
Mrs Worthington,
Sweet
Mrs Worthington,
Don't put your daughter on the stage.

Don't put your daughter on the stage, Mrs Worthington,
Don't put your daughter on the stage,
She's a bit of an ugly duckling
You must honestly confess,
And the width of her seat
Would surely defeat
Her chances of success,

12

It's a loud voice, and though it's not exactly flat,
She'll need a little more than that
To earn a living wage.
On my knees,
Mrs Worthington,
Please
Mrs Worthington,
Don't put your daughter on the stage.

Don't put your daughter on the stage, Mrs Worthington,
Don't put your daughter on the stage,
Though they said at the school of acting
She was lovely as Peer Gynt,
I'm afraid on the whole
An ingénue role
Would emphasize her squint,
She's a big girl, and though her teeth are fairly good
She's not the type I ever would
Be eager to engage,
No more buts,
Mrs Worthington,
NUTS,
Mrs Worthington,
Don't put your daughter on the stage.

Don't put your daughter on the stage, Mrs Worthington,
Don't put your daughter on the stage,
One look at her bandy legs should prove
She hasn't got a chance,
In addition to which
The son of bitch
Can neither sing nor dance,
She's a *vile* girl and uglier than mortal sin,
One look at her has put me in
A tearing bloody rage,
That sufficed,
Mrs Worthington,
Christ!
Mrs Worthington,
Don't put your daughter on the stage.

LIMERICK
Anon (LL)

There were three little owls in a wood,
Who sang hymns whenever they could.
What the words were about,
One could never make out,
But one felt it was doing them good.

HENRY KING WHO CHEWED BITS OF STRING, AND WAS EARLY CUT OFF IN DREADFUL AGONIES
Hilaire Belloc (LM)

The Chief Defect of Henry King
   Was chewing little bits of String.
At last he swallowed some which tied
   Itself in ugly Knots inside.
Physicians of the Utmost Fame
Were called at once; but when they came
They answered, as they took their Fees,
'There is no Cure for this Disease.
Henry will very soon be dead.'
His Parents stood about his Bed
Lamenting his untimely Death,
When Henry, with his Latest Breath,
Cried – 'Oh, my Friends, be warned by me,
That Breakfast, Dinner, Lunch and Tea
Are all the Human Frame requires . . .'
With that, the Wretched Child expires.

COMMENT
Dorothy Parker (LL)

Oh, life is a glorious cycle of song,
A medley of extemporanea;
And love is a thing that can never go wrong;
And I am Marie of Roumania.

HOW DOTH . . .
Lewis Carroll (HL)

How doth the little crocodile
Improve his shining tail,
And pour the waters of the Nile
On every golden scale!

How cheerfully he seems to grin,
How neatly spreads his claws,
And welcomes little fishes in
With gently smiling jaws!

FATHER WILLIAM
Lewis Carroll (LM)

'You are old, Father William,' the young man said,
'And your hair has become very white;
And yet you incessantly stand on your head –
Do you think, at your age, it is right?'

'In my youth,' Father William replied to his son,
'I feared it might injure the brain;
But, now that I'm perfectly sure I have none,
Why, I do it again and again.'

'You are old,' said the youth, 'as I mentioned before,
And have grown most uncommonly fat;
Yet you turned a back-somersault in at the door –
Pray, what is the reason of that?'

'In my youth,' said the sage, as he shook his grey locks,
'I kept all my limbs very supple
By the use of this ointment – one shilling the box –
Allow me to sell you a couple?'

'You are old,' said the youth, 'and your jaws are too weak
For anything tougher than suet;
Yet you finished the goose, with the bones and the beak –
Pray, how did you manage to do it?'

'In my youth,' said his father, 'I took to the law,
And argued each case with my wife;
And the muscular strength, which it gave to my jaw,
Has lasted the rest of my life.'

'You are old,' said the youth, 'one would hardly suppose
That your eye was as steady as ever;
Yet you balanced an eel on the end of your nose –
What made you so awfully clever?'

'I have answered three questions, and that is enough,'
Said his father; 'don't give yourself airs!
Do you think I can listen all day to such stuff?
Be off, or I'll kick you down stairs!'

MISS OTIS REGRETS
Cole Porter (MM)

Miss Otis regrets she's unable to lunch today,
Madam,
Miss Otis regrets she's unable to lunch today.
She is sorry to be delayed,
But last evening down in lovers' lane she strayed,
Madam,
Miss Otis regrets she's unable to lunch today.
When she woke up and found
That her dream of love was gone,
Madam,
She ran to the man
Who had led her so far astray,
And from under her velvet gown
She drew a gun and shot her lover down,
Madam,
Miss Otis regrets she's unable to lunch today.
When the mob came and got her
And dragged her from the jail,
Madam,
They strung her upon
The old willow across the way,
And the moment before she died
She lifted up her lovely head and cried,
Madam,
'Miss Otis regrets she's unable to lunch today.'

SHE WAS POOR BUT SHE WAS HONEST
Anon (LL)

She was poor but she was honest,
Victim of a rich man's game;
First he loved her, then he left her,
And she lost her maiden name.

Then she hastened up to London,
For to hide her grief and shame;
There she met another rich man,
And she lost her name again.

See her riding in her carriage,
In the Park and all so gay;
All the nibs and nobby persons
Come to pass the time of day.

See them at the gay theáter
Sitting in the costly stalls;
With one hand she holds the programme,
With the other strokes his hand.

See him have her dance in Paris
In her frilly underclothes;
All those Frenchies there applauding
While she strikes a striking pose.

See the little country village
Where her aged parents live;
Though they drink champagne she sends them,
Still they never can forgive.

In the rich man's arms she flutters
Like a bird with a broken wing;
First he loved her, then he left her,
And she hasn't got a ring.

See him in his splendid mansion
Entertaining with the best,
While the girl as he has ruined
Entertains a sordid guest.

See him riding in his carriage
Past the gutter where she stands;
He has made a stylish marriage
While she wrings her ringless hands.

See him in the House of Commons
Passing laws to put down crime,
While the victim of his passions
Slinks away to hide her shame.

See her on the bridge at midnight
Crying, 'Farewell, faithless love!'
There's a scream, a splash – Good Heavens!
What is she a-doing of?

Then they dragged her from the river,
Water from her clothes they wrung;
They all thought that she was drownded,
But the corpse got up and sung:

'It's the same the whole world over;
It's the poor as gets the blame,
It's the rich as gets the pleasure –
Ain't it all a bleedin' shame!'

FIRST FIG
Edna St Vincent Millay (MM)

My candle burns at both ends;
It will not last the night;
But ah, my foes, and oh, my friends –
It gives a lovely light!

ENGLISH WEATHER
Wendy Cope (HL)

January's grey and slushy,
February's chill and drear,
March is wild and wet and windy,
April seldom brings much cheer.
In May, a day or two of sunshine,
Three or four in June, perhaps.
July is usually filthy,
August skies are open taps.
In September things start dying,
Then comes cold October mist.
November we make plans to spend
The best part of December pissed.

PEAS
Anon (LL)

I always eat peas with honey,
I've done it all my life,
They do taste kind of funny,
But it keeps them on the knife.

BUSTS AND BOSOMS HAVE I KNOWN
Anon (LM)

Busts and bosoms have I known
Of various shapes and sizes
From grievous disappointments
To jubilant surprises.

Programme 3

THE BRITISH JOURNALIST
Humbert Wolfe (LM)

You cannot hope
To bribe or twist
(Thank God!) the British
Journalist;
But, seeing what
The man will do
Unbribed, there's no
Occasion to.

POLLY PERKINS
Harry Clifton (HL)

I am a broken-hearted milkman, in grief I am arrayed,
Through keeping of the company of a young servant maid,
Who lived on board and wages the house to keep clean
In a gentleman's family near Paddington Green.

Chorus
She was as beautiful as a butterfly
And as proud as a Queen
Was pretty little Polly Perkins of
Paddington Green.

She'd an ankle like an antelope and a step like a deer,
A voice like a blackbird, so mellow and clear,
Her hair hung in ringlets so beautiful and long,
I thought that she loved me but I found I was wrong.

When I'd rattle in a morning and cry 'milk below',
At the sound of my milk-cans her face she would show
With a smile upon her countenance and a laugh in her eye,
If I thought she'd have loved me, I'd have laid down to die.

21

When I asked her to marry me she said 'Oh! what stuff',
And told me to 'drop it, for she had quite enough
Of my nonsense' – at the same time I'd been very kind,
But to marry a milkman she didn't feel inclined.

'Oh, the man that has me must have silver and gold,
A chariot to ride in and be handsome and bold,
His hair must be curly as any watch spring,
And his whiskers as big as a brush for clothing.'

The words that she uttered went straight through my heart,
I sobbed, I sighed, and straight did depart;
With a tear on my eyelid as big as a bean,
Bidding good-bye to Polly and Paddington Green.

In six months she married – this hard-hearted girl –
But it was not a Wi-count, and it was not a Nearl,
It was not a 'Baronite', but a shade or two wuss,
It was a bow-legged conductor of a twopenny bus.

TENDER-HEARTEDNESS
Harry Graham (MM)

Billy, in one of his nice new sashes,
Fell in the fire and was burned to ashes;
Now, although the room grows chilly,
I haven't the heart to poke poor Billy.

ONE PERFECT ROSE
Dorothy Parker (LL)

A single flow'r he sent me, since we met.
All tenderly his messenger he chose;
Deep-hearted, pure, with scented dew still wet –
One perfect rose.

I knew the language of the floweret;
'My fragile leaves,' it said, 'his heart enclose.'
Love long has taken for his amulet
One perfect rose.

Why is it no one ever sent me yet
One perfect limousine, do you suppose?
Ah no, it's always just my luck to get
One perfect rose.

MAD DOGS AND ENGLISHMEN
Noël Coward (LM)

In tropical climes there are certain times of day
When all the citizens retire
To tear their clothes off and perspire.
It's one of those rules that the greatest fools obey,
Because the sun is much too sultry
And one must avoid its ultry-violet ray.

Papalaka papalaka papalaka boo,
Papalaka papalaka papalaka boo,
Digariga digariga digariga doo
Digariga digariga digariga doo.

The natives grieve when the white men leave their huts,
Because they're obviously definitely nuts!

Mad dogs and Englishmen
Go out in the midday sun,
The Japanese don't care to.
The Chinese wouldn't dare to,
Hindoos and Argentines sleep firmly from twelve to one.
But Englishmen detest a siesta.
In the Philippines
There are lovely screens
To protect you from the glare.
In the Malay States
There are hats like plates
Which the Britishers won't wear.
At twelve noon
The natives swoon
And no further work is done.
But mad dogs and Englishmen
Go out in the midday sun.

It's such a surprise for the Eastern eyes to see
That though the English are effete,
They're quite impervious to heat,
When the white man rides every native hides in glee,
Because the simple creatures hope he
Will impale his solar topee on a tree.

Bolyboly bolyboly bolyboly bolyboly baa,
Bolyboly bolyboly bolyboly baa,
Habaninny habaninny habaninny haa,
Habaninny habaninny habaninny haa.

It seems such a shame
When the English claim
The earth
That they give rise to such hilarity and mirth.

Mad dogs and Englishmen
Go out in the midday sun.
The toughest Burmese bandit
Can never understand it.
In Rangoon the heat of noon
Is just what the natives shun.
They put their Scotch or Rye down
And lie down.
In a jungle town
Where the sun beats down
To the rage of man and beast
The English garb
Of the English sahib
Merely gets a bit more creased.
In Bangkok
At twelve o'clock
They foam at the mouth and run,
But mad dogs and Englishmen
Go out in the midday sun.

Mad dogs and Englishmen
Go out in the midday sun.
The smallest Malay rabbit
Deplores this stupid habit.
In Hongkong
They strike a gong
And fire off a noonday gun
To reprimand each inmate
Who's in late.
In the mangrove swamps
Where the python romps
There is peace from twelve till two.

Even caribous
Lie around and snooze,
For there's nothing else to do.
In Bengal
To move at all
Is seldom, if ever done,
But mad dogs and Englishmen
Go out in the midday sun.

INDIAN SUMMER
Dorothy Parker (MM)

In youth, it was a way I had
To do my best to please,
And change, with every passing lad,
To suit his theories.

But now I know the things I know,
And do the things I do;
And if you do not like me so,
To hell, my love, with you!

DISCRETION
Roger McGough (HL)

Discretion is the better part of Valerie
though all of her is nice
lips as warm as strawberries
eyes as cold as ice
the very best of everything
only will suffice
not for her potatoes
and puddings made of rice

Not for her potatoes
and puddings made of rice
she takes carbohydrates
like God takes advice
a surfeit of ambition
is her particular vice
Valerie fondles lovers
like a mousetrap fondles mice

And though in the mornin
she may whisper: 'it was nice'
you can tell by her demeanour
that she keeps her love on ice
but you've lost your hardearned heart
now you'll have to pay the price
for she'll kiss you on the memory
and vanish in a trice

Valerie is corruptible
but known to be discreet
Valerie rides a silver cloud
where once she walked the street

WASTE
Harry Graham (LM)

I had written to Aunt Maud,
Who was on a trip abroad,
When I heard she'd died of cramp
Just too late to save the stamp.

BE PREPARED
Tom Lehrer (HL)

Be prepared!
That's the Boy Scouts' marching song,
Be prepared!
As through life you march along.
Be prepared to hold your liquor pretty well.
Don't write naughty words on walls if you can't spell.
Be prepared!
To hide that pack of cigarettes,
Don't make book if you cannot cover bets.
Keep those reefers hidden where you're sure that they will
    not be found,
And be careful not to smoke them when the scout-master's
    around,
For he will only insist that they be shared.
Be prepared!

Be prepared!
That's the Boy Scouts' solemn creed,
Be prepared!
And be clean in word and deed.
Don't solicit for your sister, that's not nice,
Unless you get a good percentage of her price.
Be prepared!
And be careful not to do
Your good deeds when there's no one watching you.
If you're looking for adventure of a new and diff'rent kind,
And you come across a Girl Scout who is similarly inclined,
Don't be nervous, don't be flustered, don't be scared.
Be prepared!

THE HORSE
Naomi Royde Smith (MM)

I know two things about the horse,
And one of them is rather coarse.

IN A BATH TEASHOP
John Betjeman (LL)

'Let us not speak, for the love we bear one another –
Let us hold hands and look.'
She, such a very ordinary little woman;
He, such a thumping crook;
But both, for a moment, little lower than the angels
In the teashop's ingle-nook.

THE PIG
Anon (LM)

It was an evening in November,
As I very well remember,
I was strolling down the street in drunken pride,
But my knees were all a-flutter,
And I landed in the gutter
And a pig came up and lay down by my side.

Yes, I lay there in the gutter
Thinking thoughts I could not utter,
When a colleen passing by did softly say
'You can tell a man who boozes
by the company he chooses' –
And the pig got up and slowly walked away.

Programme 4

A SUBALTERN'S LOVE-SONG
John Betjeman (HL)

Miss J. Hunter Dunn, Miss J Hunter Dunn,
Furnish'd and burnish'd by Aldershot sun,
What strenuous singles we played after tea,
We in the tournament – you against me!

Love-thirty, love-forty, oh! weakness of joy,
The speed of a swallow, the grace of a boy,
With carefullest carelessness, gaily you won,
I am weak from your loveliness, Joan Hunter Dunn.

Miss Joan Hunter Dunn, Miss Joan Hunter Dunn,
How mad I am, sad I am, glad that you won.
The warm-handled racket is back in its press,
But my shock-headed victor, she loves me no less.

Her father's euonymus shines as we walk,
And swing past the summer-house, buried in talk,
And cool the verandah that welcomes us in
To the six-o'clock news and a lime-juice and gin.

The scent of the conifers, sound of the bath,
The view from my bedroom of moss-dappled path,
As I struggle with double-end evening tie,
For we dance at the Golf Club, my victor and I.

On the floor of her bedroom lie blazer and shorts
And the cream-coloured walls are be-trophied with sports,
And westering, questioning settles the sun
On your low-leaded window, Miss Joan Hunter Dunn.

The Hillman is waiting, the light's in the hall,
The pictures of Egypt are bright on the wall,
My sweet, I am standing beside the oak stair
And there on the landing's the light on your hair.

By roads 'not adopted', by woodlanded ways,
She drove to the club in the late summer haze,
Into nine-o'clock Camberley, heavy with bells
And mushroomy, pine-woody, evergreen smells.

Miss Joan Hunter Dunn, Miss Joan Hunter Dunn,
I can hear from the car-park the dance has begun.
Oh! full Surrey twilight! importunate band!
Oh! strongly adorable tennis-girl's hand!

Around us are Rovers and Austins afar,
Above us, the intimate roof of the car,
And here on my right is the girl of my choice,
With the tilt of her nose and the chime of her voice,

And the scent of her wrap, and the words never said,
And the ominous, ominous dancing ahead.
We sat in the car-park till twenty to one
And now I'm engaged to Miss Joan Hunter Dunn.

LIMERICK
Anon (LM)

There was a young lady of Kent
Who said that she knew what it meant
When men asked her to dine,
Gave her cocktails and wine:
She knew what it meant, but she went.

A HAND IN THE BIRD
Roald Dahl (MM)

I am a maiden who is forty,
And a maiden I shall stay.
There are some who call me haughty,
But I care not what they say.

I was running the tombola
At our church bazaar today,
And doing it with gusto
In my usual jolly way . . .

When suddenly, I knew not why,
There came a funny feeling
Of something *crawling up my thigh*!
I nearly hit the ceiling!

A mouse! I thought. How foul! How mean!
How exquisitely tickly!
Quite soon I know I'm going to scream.
I've got to catch it quickly.

I made a grab. I caught the mouse,
Now right inside my knickers.
A mouse my foot! It was a HAND!
Great Scott! It was the vicar's!

CHOIR BOYS' SONG
Noël Coward (HL)

We're six dirty little choir boys
With really frightful minds,
We scream and shout and rush about
And pinch our friends' behinds.
Nobody could admire boys
With dirty hands and knees,
But the countryside rejoices
At our sweet soprano voices,
So we do what we damn well please.

33

SOCIAL NOTE
Dorothy Parker (LL)

Lady, lady, should you meet
One whose ways are all discreet,
One who murmurs that his wife
Is the lodestar of his life,
One who keeps assuring you
That he never was untrue,
Never loved another one . . .
Lady, lady, better run!

THE LAZIEST GAL IN TOWN
Cole Porter (LL)

I've a beau, his name is Jim,
He loves me and I love him,
But he tells me I'm too prim,
That means I'm too slow.
I let him rant, I let him rave,
I let him muss my permanent wave,
But when he says, 'Let's Misbehave,'
My reply is 'No!'

It's not 'cause I wouldn't,
It's not 'cause I shouldn't,
And, Lord knows, it's not 'cause I couldn't,
It's simply because I'm the laziest gal in town.
My poor heart is achin'
To bring home the bacon,
And if I'm alone and forsaken,
It's simply because I'm the laziest gal in town.
Though I'm more than willing to learn
How these gals get money to burn,
Ev'ry proposition I turn down,
'Way down,
It's not 'cause I wouldn't,
It's not 'cause I shouldn't,
And, Lord knows, it's not 'cause I couldn't,
It's simply because I'm the laziest gal in town.

WISHES OF AN ELDERLY MAN
Walter Raleigh (LM)

I wish I loved the Human Race;
I wish I loved its silly face;
I wish I loved the way it walks;
I wish I loved the way it talks;
And when I'm introduced to one
I wish I thought *What Jolly Fun!*

THE SPIDER AND THE FLY
Mary Howitt (MM)

'Will you walk into my parlour?' said the Spider to the Fly,
''Tis the prettiest little parlour that ever you did spy;
The way into my parlour is up a winding stair,
And I have many curious things to show when you are
    there.'

'I'm sure you must be weary, dear, with soaring up so high;
Will you rest upon my little bed?' said the Spider to the Fly.
'There are pretty curtains drawn around, the sheets are fine
    and thin;
And if you like to rest awhile, I'll snugly tuck you in!'
'Oh no, no,' said the little Fly, 'for I've often heard it said,
They never, never wake again, who sleep upon your bed!'

'Sweet creature,' said the Spider, 'you're witty and you're
    wise;
How handsome are your gauzy wings, how brilliant are your
    eyes!
I have a little looking-glass upon my parlour shelf,
If you'll step in a moment, dear, you shall behold yourself.'
'I thank you, gentle sir,' she said, 'for what you're pleased to
    say,
And bidding you good morning now, I'll call another day.'

The Spider turned him round about, and went into his den,
For well he knew the silly Fly would soon come back again;
So he wove a subtle web, in a little corner sly,

And set his table ready, to dine upon the Fly.
Then he came out to his door again and merrily did sing;
'Come hither, hither, pretty Fly, with the pearl and silver
    wing;
Your robes are green and purple – there's a crest upon your
    head;
Your eyes are like the diamond bright, but mine are dull as
    lead.'

Alas, alas! how very soon this silly little Fly,
Hearing his wily, flattering words, came slowly flitting by;
With buzzing wings she hung aloft, then near and nearer
    drew,
Thinking only of her brilliant eyes, and green and purple
    hue;
Thinking only of her crested head – poor foolish thing! At
    last,
Up jumped the cunning Spider, and fiercely held her fast.
He dragged her up his winding stair, into his dismal den,
Within his little parlour – but she ne'er came out again!

ALICE IS AT IT AGAIN
Noël Coward (LL)

In a dear little village remote and obscure
A beautiful maiden resided,
As to whether or not her intentions were pure
Opinion was sharply divided.
She loved to lie out 'neath the darkening sky
And allow the soft breeze to entrance her,
She whispered her dreams to the birds flying by
But seldom received any answer.

Over the field and along the lane
Gentle Alice would love to stray,
When it came to the end of the day,
She would wander away unheeding,
Dreaming her innocent dreams she strolled
Quite unaffected by heat or cold,
Frequently freckled or soaked with rain,

Alice was out in the lane.
Whom she met there
Every day there
Was a question answered by none,
But she'd get there
And she'd stay there
Till whatever she did was undoubtedly done.
Over the field and along the lane
When her parents had called in vain,
Sadly, sorrowfully, they'd complain,
'Alice is at it again.'

Though that dear little village
Surrounded by trees
Had neither a school nor a college
Gentle Alice acquired from the birds and the bees
Some exceedingly practical knowledge.
The curious secrets that nature revealed
She refused to allow to upset her
But she thought when observing the beasts of the field
That things might have been organised better.

Over the field and along the lane
Gentle Alice one summer's day
Met a man who was driving a dray
And he whisked her away to London.
Then, after many a year had passed,
Alice returned to her home at last
Wearing some pearls and a velvet train,
Bearing a case of champagne.
They received her
Fairly coldly
But when wine had lifted the blight
They believed her
When she boldly
Said the Salvation Army had shown her the light.
When she had left by the evening train
Both her parents in grief and pain
Murmured brokenly, 'More champagne –
Alice is at it again!'

Over the field and along the lane

Gentle Alice would make up
And take up – her stand
The road was not exactly arterial
But it led to a town near by
Where quite a lot of masculine material
Caught her roving eye.
She was ready to hitchhike
Cadillac or motor-bike,
She wasn't proud or choosey,
All she
Was aiming to be
Was a prinked up,
Minked up
Fly-by-night Floosie.
When old Rajahs
Gave her pearls as large as
Nuts on a chestnut tree
All she said was, 'Fiddlededee,
The wages of sin will be the death of me!'
Over the field and along the lane
Gentle Alice's parents would wait hand in hand.
Her dear old white-headed mother wistfully sipping
    champagne
Said, 'We've spoiled our child – spared the rod,
Open up the caviar and say Thank God,
We've got no cause to complain,
Alice is at it,
Alice is at it,
Alice is at it again.'

LIMERICK
Anon (LM)

Winter is here with his grouch,
The time when you sneeze and you slouch;
You can't take your women
Canoein' or swimmin',
But a lot can be done on a couch.

Programme 5

TEETH
Spike Milligan (LM)

English Teeth, English Teeth!
Shining in the sun
A part of British heritage
Aye, each and every one.

English Teeth, English Teeth!
Always having fun
Clamping down on bits of fish
And sausages half done.

English Teeth! HEROES' Teeth!
Hear them click! and clack!
Let's sing a song of praise to them –
Three Cheers for the Brown Grey and Black.

STATELY AS A GALLEON
Joyce Grenfell (MM)

My neighbour, Mrs Fanshaw, is portly-plump and gay,
She must be over sixty-seven, if she is a day.
You might have thought her life was dull,
It's one long whirl instead.
I asked her all about it, and this is what she said:

I've joined an Olde Thyme Dance Club, the trouble is that
    there
Are too many ladies over, and no gentlemen to spare.
It seems a shame, it's not the same,
But still it has to be,
Some ladies have to dance together,
One of them is me.

39

Stately as a galleon, I sail across the floor,
Doing the Military Two-step, as in the days of yore.
I dance with Mrs Tiverton; she's light on her feet, in spite
Of turning the scale at fourteen stone, and being of medium
    height.
So gay the band,
So giddy the sight,
Full evening dress is a must,
But the zest goes out of a beautiful waltz
When you dance it bust to bust.

So, stately as two galleons, we sail across the floor,
Doing the Valse Valeta as in the days of yore.
The gent is Mrs Tiverton, I am her lady fair,
She bows to me ever so nicely and I curtsey to her with care.
So gay the band,
So giddy the sight,
But it's not the same in the end
For a lady is never a gentleman, though
She may be your bosom friend.

So, stately as a galleon, I sail across the floor,
Doing the dear old Lancers, as in the days of yore.
I'm led by Mrs Tiverton, she swings me round and round
And though she manoeuvres me wonderfully well
I never get off the ground.
So gay the band,
So giddy the sight,
I try not to get depressed.
And it's done me a power of good to explode,
And get this lot off my chest.

COME. AND BE MY BABY
Maya Angelou (LL)

The highway is full of big cars
going nowhere fast
And folks is smoking anything that'll burn
Some people wrap their lives around a cocktail glass
And you sit wondering
Where you're going to turn
I got it.
Come. And be my baby.

Some prophets say the world is gonna end tomorrow
But others say we've got a week or two
The paper is full of every kind of blooming horror
And you sit wondering
What you're gonna do.
I got it.
Come. And be my baby.

LIMERICK
Ogden Nash (LM)

There was an old man in a trunk
Who inquired of his wife, 'Am I drunk?'
She replied with regret,
'I'm afraid so, my pet.'
And he answered, 'It's just as I thunk.'

THE PELICAN
Anon (HL)

What a wonderful beast is the Pelican!
Whose bill can hold more than his belly can.
He can take in his beak
Enough food for a week –
I'm damned if I know how the hell he can.

LIMERICK
Anon (MM)

There was an old maid of Duluth
Who wept when she thought of her youth,
And the glorious chances
She'd missed at school dances,
And once in a telephone booth.

THE ROLLING ENGLISH ROAD
G. K. Chesterton (LM)

Before the Roman came to Rye or out to Severn strode,
The rolling English drunkard made the rolling English road.
A reeling road, a rolling road, that rambles round the shire,
And after him the parson ran, the sexton and the squire;
A merry road, a mazy road, and such as we did tread
That night we went to Birmingham by way of Beachy Head.

I knew no harm of Bonaparte and plenty of the Squire,
And for to fight the Frenchmen I did not much desire;
But I did bash their baggonets because they came arrayed
To straighten out the crooked road an English drunkard
made,
Where you and I went down the lane with ale-mugs in our
hands,
The night we went to Glastonbury by way of Goodwin
Sands.

His sins they were forgiven him; or why do flowers run
Behind him; and the hedges all strengthening in the sun?
The wild thing went from left to right and knew not which
was which,
But the wild rose was above him when they found him in
the ditch.
God pardon us, nor harden us; we did not see so clear
The night we went to Bannockburn by way of Brighton
Pier.

My friends, we will not go again or ape an ancient rage,
Or stretch the folly of our youth to be the shame of age,
But walk with clearer eyes and ears this path that wandereth,
And see undrugged in evening light the decent inn of death;
For there is good news yet to hear and fine things to be seen,
Before we go to Paradise by way of Kensal Green.

MARY, MARY
Roald Dahl (LL)

Mary, Mary, quite contrary,
How does your garden grow?
'I live with my brat in a high-rise flat,
So how in the world would I know.'

A PENNILESS FRENCH MOUSE
Jeremy Lloyd (MM)

A penniless French mouse called Jacques,
In beret, boots and belted mac,
Strode idly down an empty drain
Protected 'gainst the wind and rain,
When from a grating in the street
A cigarette fell at his feet,
And in surprise, he cried:
'Mon Dieu!
It is my favourite brand,
Disque Bleu.
Ma foi, these are très fort,' he said.
Inhaling deep, the end glowed red.
A smell, he thought, was just le drain,
Was gas escaping from le main.
Le grande explosion, au r'voir Jacques,
In beret, boots and belted mac.

And now he has gone
To the great mousehole in the sky,
Where mountains of le cheese
Stretch away as far as the eye can see.
'Excusez-moi, monsieur . . .'
'Oui?'
'Which way to le roquefort s'il vous plait?'

LIMERICK
Veronica Nicholson (LM)

I once took my girl to Southend,
Intending a loving weekend;
But imagine the fuss –
In the room next to us
Was my wife with a gentleman friend.

CHARLES AUGUSTUS FORTESCUE WHO ALWAYS DID WHAT WAS RIGHT, AND SO ACCUMULATED AN IMMENSE FORTUNE
Hilaire Belloc (LL)

The nicest child I ever knew
Was Charles Augustus Fortescue.
He never lost his cap, or tore
His stockings or his pinafore:
In eating Bread he made no Crumbs,
He was extremely fond of sums,
To which, however, he preferred
The Parsing of a Latin Word –
He sought, when it was in his power,
For information twice an hour,
And as for finding Mutton-Fat
Unappetising, far from that!
He often, at his Father's Board,
Would beg them, of his own accord,
To give him, if they did not mind,
The Greasiest Morsels they could find –
His Later Years did not belie
The Promise of his Infancy.
In Public Life he always tried
To take a judgment Broad and Wide;
In Private, none was more than he
Renowned for quiet courtesy.
He rose at once in his Career,
And long before his Fortieth Year
Had wedded Fifi, Only Child
Of Bunyan, First Lord Aberfylde.
He thus became immensely Rich,
And built the Splendid Mansion which
Is called 'The Cedars, Muswell Hill',
Where he resides in Affluence still
To show what everybody might
Become by SIMPLY DOING RIGHT.

RÉSUMÉ
Dorothy Parker (MM)

Razors pain you:
Rivers are damp:
Acids stain you:
And drugs cause cramp.
Guns aren't lawful:
Nooses give:
Gas smells awful:
You might as well live.

THE HORSE'S FAREWELL TO HIS COWBOY
Pam Ayres (LM)

Farewell to you cowboy, my day it is done,
Of rounding up cows in the heat of the sun
Of roping the dogies and branding the steer
And having your gun going off in my ear.
I galloped the prairie without any thanks
Your great silver spurs in my bony old flanks
And I've seen many things in my life it is true
But never a cowboy more stupid than you.

Cowboy can you hear me inside the saloon?
I'm waiting out here in the light of the moon,
My hardworking days they are past and gone by,
And I'm bound for the great clover field in the sky.

Farewell to the feel of your filthy old jeans
Farewell to the smell of your coffee and beans
Farewell to you in your stetson and chaps,
Cheating at poker and shooting the craps.
You rode me too fast and you rode me too far,
Mile after mile of you shouting 'Yee har!'
Hounded by outlaws away down the track,
With a gun on my tail and a berk on my back.

I never remember you treating me right,
I was tied to a cactus and hungry all night,

47

When I was weary and dying of thirst,
I always knew it was you who came first,
Well maybe you are mighty quick on the draw,
But cowboy you're slow with the fodder and straw,
Look at me pardner, I'm all skin and bone,
So tonight I ride into the sunset . . . alone

He'll have a shock when he comes out of there,
Me, with four legs sticking up in the air,
Don't say goodbye or thanks for the ride,
My friend it's too little too late. I have died.
Won't somebody lift up the old saddle flaps,
My eyes have grown weary, I'm tired of talk,
And as from tonight, he can bloody well walk.

THE PEOPLE UPSTAIRS
Ogden Nash (HL)

The people upstairs all practise ballet.
Their living room is a bowling alley.
Their bedroom is full of conducted tours.
Their radio is louder than yours.
They celebrate weekends all the week.
When they take a shower, your ceilings leak.
They try to get their parties to mix
By supplying their guests with Pogo sticks,
And when their orgy at last abates,
They go to the bathroom on roller skates.
I might love the people upstairs wondrous
If instead of above us, they just lived under us.

THE RABBIT
Anon (MM)

The rabbit has a charming face:
Its private life is a disgrace.
I really dare not name to you
The awful things that rabbits do;
Things that your paper never prints –
You only mention them in hints.
They have such lost, degraded souls
No wonder they inhabit holes;
When such depravity is found
It can only live underground.

Programme 6

LIMERICK
Anon (HL)

There was a young man from Darjeeling,
Who got on a bus bound for Ealing;
It said at the door:
'Don't spit on the floor'
So he carefully spat on the ceiling.

THE WALRUS AND THE CARPENTER
Lewis Carroll (LM)

The sun was shining on the sea,
Shining with all his might:
He did his very best to make
The billows smooth and bright –
And this was odd, because it was
The middle of the night.

The moon was shining sulkily,
Because she thought the sun
Had got no business to be there
After the day was done –
'It's very rude of him,' she said,
'To come and spoil the fun!'

The sea was wet as wet could be,
The sands were dry as dry.
You could not see a cloud, because
No cloud was in the sky:
No birds were flying overhead –
There were no birds to fly.

The Walrus and the Carpenter
Were walking close at hand:

They wept like anything to see
Such quantities of sand:
'If this were only cleared away,'
They said, 'it *would* be grand!'

'If seven maids with seven mops
Swept it for half a year,
Do you suppose,' the Walrus said,
'That they could get it clear?'
'I doubt it,' said the Carpenter,
And shed a bitter tear.

'O Oysters, come and walk with us!'
The Walrus did beseech.
'A pleasant walk, a pleasant talk,
Along the briny beach:
We cannot do with more than four,
To give a hand to each.'

The eldest Oyster looked at him,
But not a word he said:
The eldest Oyster winked his eye,
And shook his heavy head —
Meaning to say he did not choose
To leave the oyster-bed.

But four young Oysters hurried up,
All eager for the treat:
Their coats were brushed, their faces washed,
Their shoes were clean and neat —
And this was odd, because, you know,
They hadn't any feet.

Four other Oysters followed them,
And yet another four;
And thick and fast they came at last,
And more, and more, and more —
All hopping through the frothy waves,
And scrambling to the shore.

The Walrus and the Carpenter
Walked on a mile or so,

And then they rested on a rock
Conveniently low:
And all the little Oysters stood
And waited in a row.

'The time has come,' the Walrus said,
'To talk of many things:
Of shoes – and ships – and sealing wax –
Of cabbages – and kings –
And why the sea is boiling hot –
And whether pigs have wings.'

'But wait a bit,' the Oysters cried,
'Before we have our chat;
For some of us are out of breath,
And all of us are fat!'
'No hurry!' said the Carpenter.
They thanked him much for that.

'A loaf of bread,' the Walrus said,
'Is what we chiefly need:
Pepper and vinegar besides
Are very good indeed –
Now, if you're ready, Oysters dear,
We can begin to feed.'

'But not on us!' the Oysters cried,
Turning a little blue.
'After such kindness that would be
A dismal thing to do!'
'The night is fine,' the Walrus said,
'Do you admire the view?'

'It was so kind of you to come,
And you are very nice!'
The Carpenter said nothing but
'Cut us another slice.
I wish you were not quite so deaf –
I've had to ask you twice!'

'It seems a shame,' the Walrus said,
'To play them such a trick.

After we've brought them out so far,
And made them trot so quick!'
The Carpenter said nothing but
'The butter's spread too thick!'

'I weep for you,' the Walrus said:
'I deeply sympathise.'
With sobs and tears he sorted out
Those of the largest size,
Holding his pocket-handkerchief
Before his streaming eyes.

'O Oysters,' said the Carpenter,
'You've had a pleasant run!
Shall we be trotting home again?'
But answer came there none –
And this was scarcely odd, because
They'd eaten every one.

THIS ENGLISHWOMAN
Stevie Smith (MM)

This Englishwoman is so refined
She has no bosom and no behind.

UNFORTUNATE COINCIDENCE
Dorothy Parker (LL)

By the time you swear you're his
Shivering and sighing,
And he vows his passion is
Infinite, undying –
Lady, make a note of this:
One of you is lying.

THE PIG
Spike Milligan (HL)

A very rash young lady pig
(They say she was a smasher)
Suddenly ran
Under a van –
Now she's a gammon rasher.

LET'S DO IT
Noël Coward (MM)

Mr Irving Berlin
Often emphasizes sin
In a charming way.
Mr Coward we know
Wrote a song or two to show
Sex was here to stay.
Richard Rodgers it's true
Takes a more romantic view
Of that sly biological urge.
But it really was Cole
Who contrived to make the whole
Thing merge.

He said that Belgians and Dutch do it,
Even Hildegarde and Hutch do it,
Let's do it, let's fall in love.
Monkeys when ever you look do it,
Aly Khan and King Farouk do it,
Let's do it, let's fall in love.
The most recherché cocottes do it
In a luxury flat,
Locks, Dunns and Scotts do it
At the drop of a hat,
Excited spinsters in spas do it,
Duchesses when opening bazaars do it,
Let's do it, let's fall in love.

Our leading writers in swarms do it,
Somerset and all the Maughams do it,
Let's do it, let's fall in love.
The Brontës felt that they must do it,
Mrs Humphrey Ward could just do it,
Let's do it, let's fall in love.
Anouilh and Sartre – God knows why – do it,
As a sort of a curse
Eliot and Fry do it,
But they do it in verse.
Some mystics, as a routine do it,
Even Evelyn Waugh and Graham Greene do it,

Let's do it, let's fall in love.

In the Spring of the year
Inhibitions disappear
And our hearts beat high,
We had better face facts
Every gland that overacts
Has an alibi,
For each bird and each bee,
Each slap-happy sappy tree,
Each temptation that lures us along
Is just Nature elle-même
Merely singing us the same
Old song.

Girls from the RADA do it,
BBC announcers may do it,
Let's do it, let's fall in love.
The Ballet Jooss to a man do it,
Alfred Lunt and Lynn Fontanne do it,
Let's do it, let's fall in love.
My kith and kin, more or less, do it,
Every uncle and aunt,
But I confess to it,
I've one cousin who can't.
Critics as sour as quince do it,
Even Emile Littler and Prince do it,
Let's do it, let's fall in love.

The House of Commons en bloc do it,
Civil Servants by the clock do it,
Let's do it, let's fall in love
Deacons who've done it before do it,
Minor canons with a roar do it,
Let's do it, let's fall in love.
Some rather rorty old rips do it
When they get a bit tight,
Government Whips do it
If it takes them all night,
Old mountain goats in ravines do it,
Probably we'll live to see machines do it,
Let's do it, let's fall in love.

ALGY
Anon (LM)

Algy met a bear
A bear met Algy
The bear was bulgy
The bulge was Algy

CELIA CELIA
Adrian Mitchell (HL)

When I am sad and weary
When I think all hope is gone
When I walk along High Holborn
I think of you with nothing on.

THE PHYSICIAN
Cole Porter (LL)

Once I loved such a shattering physician,
Quite the best-looking doctor in the state.
He looked after my physical condition,
And his bedside manner was great.
When I'd gaze up and see him there above me,
Looking less like a doctor than a Turk,
I was tempted to whisper, 'Do you love me,
Or do you merely love your work?'

He said my bronchial tubes were entrancing,
My epiglottis filled him with glee,
He simply loved my larynx
And went wild about my pharynx,
But he never said he loved me.
He said my epidermis was darling,
And found my blood as blue as could be,
He went through wild ecstatics,
When I showed him my lymphatics,
But he never said he loved me.
And though, no doubt,
It was not very smart of me,
I kept on a-wracking my soul
To figure out
Why he loved ev'ry part of me,
And yet not me as a whole.
With my esophagus he was ravished,
Enthusiastic to a degree,
He said 'twas just enormous,
My appendix vermiformis,
But he never said he loved me.

He said my cerebellum was brilliant,
And my cerebrum far from NG,
I know he thought a lotta
My medulla oblongata,
But he never said he loved me.
He said my maxillaries were marvels,
And found my sternum stunning to see,
He did a double hurdle

59

When I shook my pelvic girdle,
But he never said he loved me.
He seemed amused
When he first made a test of me
To further his medical art,
Yet he refused
When he'd fix up the rest of me,
To cure that ache in my heart.
I know he thought my pancreas perfect,
And for my spleen was keen as could be,
He said of all his sweeties,
I'd the sweetest diabetes,
But he never said he loved me.

He said my vertebrae were 'sehr schöne,'
And called my coccyx 'plus que gentil,'
He murmured 'molto bella,'
When I sat on his patella,
But he never said he loved me.
He took a fleeting look at my thorax,
And started singing slightly off key,
He cried, 'May Heaven strike us,'
When I played my umbilicus,
But he never said he loved me.
As it was dark,
I suggested we walk about
Before he returned to his post.
Once in the park,
I induced him to talk about
The thing I wanted the most.
He lingered on with me until morning,
Yet when I tried to pay him his fee,
He said, 'Why, don't be funny,
It is I who owe you money,'
But he never said he loved me.

THE LION AND ALBERT
George Marriott Edgar (MM)

There's a famous seaside place called Blackpool,
That's noted for fresh air and fun,
And Mr and Mrs Ramsbottom
Went there with young Albert, their son.

A grand little lad was young Albert,
All dressed in his best; quite a swell
With a stick with an 'orse's 'ead 'andle,
The finest that Woolworth's could sell.

They didn't think much to the Ocean:
The waves, they was fiddlin' and small,
There was no wrecks and nobody drownded,
Fact, nothing to laugh at at all.

So, seeking for further amusement,
They paid and went into the Zoo,
Where they'd Lions and Tigers and Camels,
And old ale and sandwiches too.

There were one great big Lion called Wallace;
His nose were all covered with scars –
He lay in a somnolent posture
With the side of his face on the bars.

Now Albert had heard about Lions,
How they was ferocious and wild –
To see Wallace lying so peaceful,
Well, it didn't seem right to the child.

So straightway the brave little feller,
Not showing a morsel of fear,
Took his stick with its 'orse's 'ead 'andle
And pushed it in Wallace's ear.

You could see that the Lion didn't like it,
For giving a kind of a roll,
He pulled Albert inside the cage with 'im,
And swallowed the little lad 'ole.

Then Pa, who had seen the occurrence,
And didn't know what to do next,
Said, 'Mother! Yon Lion's 'et Albert,'
And Mother said, 'Well, I am vexed!'

Then Mr and Mrs Ramsbottom –
Quite rightly, when all's said and done –
Complained to the Animal Keeper
That the Lion had eaten their son.

The keeper was quite nice about it;
He said, 'What a nasty mishap.
Are you sure that it's *your* boy he's eaten?'
Pa said, 'Am I sure? There's his cap!'

The manager had to be sent for.
He came and he said, 'What's to do?'
Pa said 'Yon Lion's 'et Albert,
And 'im in his Sunday clothes too.'

Then Mother said, 'Right's right, young feller;
I think it's a shame and a sin
For a lion to go and eat Albert,
And after we've paid to come in.'

The manager wanted no trouble,
He took out his purse right away,
Saying 'How much to settle the matter?'
And Pa said 'What do you usually pay?'

But Mother had turned a bit awkward
When she thought where her Albert had gone.
She said 'No! someone's got to be summonsed' –
So that was decided upon.

Then off they went to the P'lice Station,
In front of the Magistrate chap;
They told 'im what happened to Albert,
And proved it by showing his cap.

The Magistrate gave his opinion
That no one was really to blame

And he said that he hoped the Ramsbottoms
Would have further sons to their name.

At that Mother got proper blazing,
'And thank you, sir, kindly,' said she.
'What, waste all our lives raising children
To feed ruddy Lions? Not me!'

Programme 7

LORD FINCHLEY
Hilaire Belloc (LM)

Lord Finchley tried to mend the Electric Light
Himself. It struck him dead: And serve him right!
It is the business of the wealthy man
To give employment to the artisan.

PRELUDE
Wendy Cope (LL)

It wouldn't be a good idea
To let him stay.
When they knew each other better –
Not today.
But she put on her new black knickers
Anyway.

I'VE BEEN TO A MARVELLOUS PARTY
Noël Coward (MM)

Quite for no reason
I'm here for the Season
And high as a kite,
Living in error
With Maud at Cap Ferrat
Which couldn't be right.
Everyone's here and frightfully gay,
Nobody cares what people say,
Though the Riviera
Seems really much queerer
Than Rome at its height,
Yesterday night –

I've been to a marvellous party
With Nounou and Nada and Nell,
It was in the fresh air
And we went as we were
And we stayed as we were
Which was Hell.
Poor Grace started singing at midnight
And didn't stop singing till four;
We knew the excitement was bound to begin
When Laura got blind on Dubonnet and gin
And scratched her veneer with a Cartier pin,
I couldn't have liked it more.

I've been to a marvellous party,
I must say the fun was intense,
We all had to do
What the people we knew
Would be doing a hundred years hence.
Dear Cecil arrived wearing armour,
Some shells and a black feather boa,
Poor Millicent wore a surrealist comb
Made of bits of mosaic from St Peter's in Rome,
But the weight was so great that she had to go home,
I couldn't have liked it more!

People's behaviour
Away from Belgravia
Would make you aghast,
So much variety
Watching Society
Scampering past,
If you have any mind at all
Gibbon's divine *Decline and Fall*
Seems pretty flimsy,
No more than a whimsy,
By way of contrast
On Saturday last —

I've been to a marvellous party,
We didn't start dinner till ten
And young Bobbie Carr
Did a stunt at the bar
With a lot of extraordinary men;
Dear Baba arrived with a turtle
Which shattered us all to the core,
The Grand Duke was dancing a foxtrot with me
When suddenly Cyril screamed Fiddledidee
And ripped off his trousers and jumped in the sea,
I couldn't have liked it more.

I've been to a marvellous party,
Elise made an entrance with May,
You'd never have guessed
From her fisherman's vest
That her bust had been whittled away.
Poor Lulu got fried on Chianti
And talked about esprit de corps.
Maurice made a couple of passes at Gus
And Freddie, who hates any kind of a fuss,
Did half the Big Apple and twisted his truss,
I couldn't have liked it more.

I've been to a marvellous party,
We played the most wonderful game,
Maureen disappeared
And came back in a beard
And we all had to guess at her name!

We talked about growing old gracefully
And Elsie who's seventy-four
Said, 'A, it's a question of being sincere,
And B, if you're supple you've nothing to fear.'
Then she swung upside down from a glass chandelier,
I couldn't have liked it more.

LIMERICK
Anon (HL)

There's a notable family named Stein,
There's Gert and there's Ep and there's Ein.
Gert's prose is all bunk,
Ep's sculpture just junk
And nobody understands Ein.

THE SONG OF THE QUOODLE
G. K. Chesterton (LM)

They haven't got no noses,
The fallen sons of Eve,
Even the smell of roses
Is not what they supposes,
But more than mind discloses,
And more than men believe.

They haven't got no noses,
They cannot even tell
When door and darkness closes
The park old Gluck encloses
Where even the Law of Moses
Will let you steal a smell.

The brilliant smell of water,
The brave smell of a stone,
The smell of dew and thunder,
The old bones buried under,
Are things in which they blunder
And err, if left alone.

The wind from winter forests,
The scent of scentless flowers,
The breath of brides' adorning,
The smell of snare and warning,
The smell of Sunday morning
God gave to us for ours.

★ ★ ★

And Quoodle here discloses
All things that Quoodle can,
They haven't got no noses,
They haven't got no noses,
And goodness only knowses
The noselessness of Man.

SYMPTOM RECITAL
Dorothy Parker (LL)

I do not like my state of mind;
I'm bitter, querulous, unkind.
I hate my legs, I hate my hands,
I do not yearn for lovelier lands,
I dread the dawn's recurrent light;
I hate to go to bed at night.
I snoot at simple, earnest folk.
I cannot take the gentlest joke.
I find no peace in paint or type.
My world is but a lot of tripe.
I'm disillusioned, empty-breasted.
For what I think I'd be arrested.
I am not sick, I am not well,
My quondam dreams are shot to hell.
My soul is crushed, my spirit sore;
I do not like me any more.
I cavil, quarrel, grumble, grouse,
I ponder on the narrow house.
I shudder at the thought of men.
I'm due to fall in love again.

A WORD OF ENCOURAGEMENT
J. R. Pope (MM)

O what a tangled web we weave
When first we practise to deceive!
But when we've practised quite a while
How vastly we improve our style!

70

MUNGOJERRIE AND RUMPELTEAZER
T. S. Eliot (HL)

Mungojerrie and Rumpelteazer were a very notorious couple
    of cats.
As knockabout clowns, quick-change comedians, tight-rope
    walkers and acrobats
They had an extensive reputation. They made their home in
    Victoria Grove –
That was merely their centre of operation, for they were
    incurably given to rove.
They were very well known in Cornwall Gardens, in
    Launceston Place and in Kensington Square –
They had really a little more reputation than a couple of cats
    can very well bear.

If the area window was found ajar
And the basement looked like a field of war,
If a tile or two came loose on the roof,
Which presently ceased to be waterproof,
If the drawers were pulled out from the bedroom chests,
And you couldn't find one of your winter vests,
Or after supper one of the girls
Suddenly missed her Woolworth pearls:
Then the family would say: 'It's that horrible cat!
It was Mungojerrie – or Rumpelteazer!' – And most of the
    time they left it at that.

Mungojerrie and Rumpelteazer had a very unusual gift of the
    gab.
They were highly efficient cat-burglars as well, and
    remarkably smart at a smash-and-grab.
They made their home in Victoria Grove. They had no
    regular occupation.
They were plausible fellows, and liked to engage a friendly
    policeman in conversation.

When the family assembled for Sunday dinner,
With their minds made up that they wouldn't get thinner
On Argentine joint, potatoes and greens,
And the cook would appear from behind the scenes
And say in a voice that was broken with sorrow:

71

'I'm afraid you must wait and have dinner *tomorrow*!
For the joint has gone from the oven – like that!'
Then the family would say: 'It's that horrible cat!
It was Mungojerrie – or Rumpelteazer!' – And most of the
    time they left it at that.

Mungojerrie and Rumpelteazer had a wonderful way of
    working together.
And some of the time you would say it was luck, and some
    of the time you would say it was weather.
They would go through the house like a hurricane, and no
    sober person could take his oath
Was it Mungojerrie – or Rumpelteazer? or could you have
    sworn that it mightn't be both?

And when you heard a dining-room smash
Or up from the pantry there came a loud crash
Or down from the library came a loud *ping*
From a vase which was commonly said to be Ming –
Then the family would say: 'Now which was which cat?
It was Mungojerrie! AND Rumpelteazer!' And there's
    nothing at all to be done about that!

AUTUMN
Stevie Smith (LM)

He told his life story to Mrs Courtly
Who was a widow. 'Let us get married shortly,'
He said. 'I am no longer passionate,
But we could have some conversation before it is too late.'

ALWAYS TRUE TO YOU IN MY FASHION
Cole Porter (MM)

Oh, Bill,
Why can't you behave,
Why can't you behave?
How in hell can you be jealous
When you know, baby, I'm your slave?
I'm just mad for you,
And I'll always be,
But naturally

If a custom-tailored vet
Asks me out for something wet,
When the vet begins to pet, I cry 'Hooray!'
But I'm always true to you, darlin', in my fashion,
Yes, I'm always true to you, darlin', in my way.
I enjoy a tender pass
By the boss of Boston, Mass.,
Though his pass is middle-class and notta Backa Bay.
But I'm always true to you, darlin', in my fashion,
Yes, I'm always true to you, darlin', in my way.
There's a madman known as Mack
Who is planning to attack,
If his mad attack means a Cadillac, okay!
But I'm always true to you, darlin', in my fashion,
Yes, I'm always true to you, darlin', in my way.

I've been asked to have a meal
By a big tycoon in steel,
If the meal includes a deal, accept I may.
But I'm always true to you, darlin', in my fashion,
Yes, I'm always true to you, darlin', in my way.
I could never curl my lip
To a dazzlin' diamond clip,
Though the clip meant 'let 'er rip,' I'd not say 'Nay!'
But I'm always true to you, darlin', in my fashion,
Yes, I'm always true to you, darlin', in my way.
There's an oil man known as Tex
Who is keen to give me checks,
And his checks, I fear, mean that sex is here to stay!
But I'm always true to you, darlin', in my fashion,

Yes, I'm always true to you, darlin', in my way.

There's a wealthy Hindu priest
Who's a wolf, to say the least,
When the priest goes too far east, I also stray.
But I'm always true to you, darlin', in my fashion,
Yes, I'm always true to you, darlin', in my way.
There's a lush from Portland, Ore.,
Who is rich but sich a bore,
When the bore falls on the floor, I let him lay.
But I'm always true to you, darlin', in my fashion,
Yes, I'm always true to you, darlin', in my way.
Mister Harris, plutocrat,
Wants to give my cheek a pat,
If the Harris pat
Means a Paris hat,
Bébé, Oo-la-la!
Mais je suis toujours fidèle, darlin', in my fashion,
Oui, je suis toujours fidèle, darlin', in my way.

From Ohio Mister Thorne
Calls me up from night 'til morn,
Mister Thorne once cornered corn and that ain't hay.
But I'm always true to you, darlin', in my fashion,
Yes, I'm always true to you, darlin', in my way.
From Milwaukee, Mister Fritz
Often moves me to the Ritz,
Mister Fritz is full of Schlitz and full of play.
But I'm always true to you, darlin', in my fashion,
Yes, I'm always true to you, darlin', in my way.
Mister Gable, I mean Clark,
Wants me on his boat to park,
If the Gable boat
Means a sable coat,
Anchors aweigh!
But I'm always true to you, darlin', in my fashion,
Yes, I'm always true to you, darlin', in my way.

REBECCA WHO SLAMMED DOORS FOR FUN AND PERISHED MISERABLY
Hilaire Belloc (LM)

A Trick that everyone abhors
In Little Girls is slamming Doors,
A Wealthy Bankers's Little Daughter
Who lived in Palace Green, Bayswater
(By name Rebecca Offendort),
Was given to this Furious Sport.

She would deliberately go
And Slam the door like Billy-Ho!
To make her Uncle Jacob start.
She was not really bad at heart,
But only rather rude and wild:
She was an aggravating child . . .

It happened that a Marble Bust
Of Abraham was standing just
Above the Door this little Lamb
Had carefully prepared to Slam,
And Down it came! It knocked her flat!
It laid her out! She looked like that.

Her funeral Sermon (which was long
And followed by a Sacred Song)
Mentioned her Virtues, it is true,
But dwelt upon her Vices too,
And showed the Dreadful End of One
Who goes and slams the door for Fun.

The children who were brought to hear
The awful Tale from far and near
Were much impressed, and inly swore
They never more would slam the Door.
 – As often they had done before.

AS I WAS GOING UP THE STAIR
Anon (MM)

As I was going up the stair,
I met a man who wasn't there,
He wasn't there again today,
I wish, I wish he'd go away.

FATIGUE
Hilaire Belloc (LM)

I'm tired of Love: I'm still more tired of Rhyme.
But Money gives me pleasure all the time.

Programme 8

PIG RHYME
Jan Morris (MM)

A mother pig crooned to her sweet little piglets three:
Come, wipe all the mud from your trotters,
   and if you are good – we'll see!
There *may* be a bucket of acorn swill for your tea!

Swill, said the piglets, acorn swill, oh wow!
Is that all you've got, you silly old sow?

The mother pig cried: But when *I* was wee,
A bucket of swill was oh, such a treat for me!
On birthdays I had it, and when I was good as could be!

Big deal, said the piglets three.

77

WHEN YOU ARE OLD AND GREY
Tom Lehrer (HL)

Since I still appreciate you
Let's find love while we may,
Because I know I'll hate you
When you are old and grey.

So say you love me here and now,
I'll make the most of that.
Say you love and trust me,
For I know you'll disgust me
When you're old and getting fat.

An awful debility, a lessened utility,
A loss of mobility is a strong possibility,
In all probability I'll lose my virility
And you, your fertility and desirability,
And this liability of total sterility
Will lead to hostility and a sense of futility,
So let's act with agility while we still have facility,
For we'll soon reach senility and lose the ability.

Your teeth will start to go, dear,
Your waist will start to spread.
In twenty years or so, dear,
I'll wish that you were dead.
I'll never love you then at all
The way I do today.
So please remember,
When I leave in December,
I told you so in May.

LOVEY-DOVEY
Anon (LL)

The dove is a symbol of love pure and true;
But say! Have you heard the things they do?
Coo!

THE COMMON CORMORANT
Christopher Isherwood (LM)

The common cormorant or shag
Lays eggs inside a paper bag
The reason you will see no doubt
It is to keep the lightning out.
But what these unobservant birds
Have never noticed is that herds
Of wandering bears may come with buns
And steal the bags to hold the crumbs.

MY BEST FRIEND
Jeremy Lloyd (LL)

Save for the humming of the bees
And raindrops falling thro' the trees,
The wood was silent as a grave
Whilst shafts of sunlight made a brave
Attempt to pierce the velvet gloom
As lonely as an empty room.
Alone was I, but not afraid,
The friend I'd been with must have strayed,
For tho' I called, no answer came
And so I played a splendid game
In the bracken wet and thick
With my favourite walking stick.
And then, a voice called out quite near:
'So there you are, old chap, come here.'
And sitting there, upon a log
Was my best friend, who said: 'Good dog.'

LIMERICK
Anon (MM)

There was a young girl of Penzance,
Who decided to take just one chance;
She let herself go
On the lap of her beau,
And now all her sisters are aunts.

JABBERWOCKY
Lewis Carroll (HL)

'Twas brillig, and the slithy toves
Did gyre and gimble in the wabe;
All mimsy were the borogroves,
And the mome raths outgrabe.

'Beware the Jabberwock, my son!
The jaws that bite, the claws that catch!
Beware the Jubjub bird and shun
The frumious Bandersnatch!'

He took his vorpal sword in hand:
Long time the manxome foe he sought –
So rested he by the Tumtum tree,
And stood awhile in thought.

And as in uffish thought he stood,
The Jabberwock, with eyes of flame,
Came whiffling through the tulgey wood,
And burbled as it came!

One, two! One, two! And through and through
The vorpal blade went snicker-snack!
He left it dead, and with its head
He went galumphing back.

'And hast thou slain the Jabberwock!
Come to my arms, my beamish boy!
O frabjous day! Callooh! Callay!'
He chortled in his joy.

'Twas brillig, and the slithy toves
Did gyre and gimble in the wabe;
All mimsy were the borogroves,
And the mome raths outgrabe.

CURL UP AND DIET
Ogden Nash (LM)

Some ladies smoke too much and some ladies drink too
   much and some ladies pray too much,
But all ladies think that they weigh too much.
They may be as slender as a sylph or a dryad,
But just let them get on the scales and they embark on a
   doleful jeremiad;
No matter how low the figure the needle happens to touch,
They always claim it is at least five pounds too much;
To the world she may appear slinky and feline,
But she inspects herself in the mirror and cries, Oh, I look
   like a sea lion.
Yes, she tells you she is growing into the shape of a sea cow
   or manatee,
And if you say No, my dear, she says you are just lying to
   make her feel better, and if you say Yes, my dear, you
   injure her vanity.
Once upon a time there was a girl more beautiful and witty
   and charming than tongue can tell,
And she is now a dangerous raving maniac in a padded cell.
And the first indication her friends and relatives had that she
   was mentally overwrought
Was one day when she said, I weigh a hundred and twenty-
   seven, which is exactly what I ought.
Oh, often I am haunted
By the thought that somebody might someday discover a diet
   that would let ladies reduce just as much as they wanted,
Because I wonder if there is a woman in the world strong-
   minded enough to shed ten pounds or twenty,
And say There now, that's plenty;
And I fear me one ten-pound loss would only arouse the
   craving for another.
So it wouldn't do any good for ladies to get their ambition
   and look like somebody's fourteen-year-old brother,
Because, having accomplished this with ease,
They would next want to look like somebody's fourteen-
   year-old brother in the final stages of some obscure
   disease,
And the more success you have the more you want to get of
   it,

So then their goal would be to look like somebody's
    fourteen-year-old brother's ghost, or rather not the ghost
    itself, which is fairly solid, but a silhouette of it.
So I think it is very nice for ladies to be lithe and lissome,
But not so much that you cut yourself if you happen to
    embrace or kissome.

I SAW A JOLLY HUNTER
Charles Causley (HL)

I saw a jolly hunter
With a jolly gun
Walking in the country
In the jolly sun

In the jolly meadow
Sat a jolly hare
Saw the jolly hunter
Took jolly care

Hunter jolly eager –
Sight of jolly prey
Forgot gun pointing
Wrong jolly way

Jolly hunter jolly head
Over heels gone.
Jolly old safety-catch
Not jolly on.

Bang went the jolly gun.
Hunter jolly dead.
Jolly hare got clean away.
Jolly good, I said.

THE STATELY HOMES OF ENGLAND
Noël Coward (MM)

Lord Elderley, Lord Borrowmere, Lord Sickert and Lord
   Camp,
With every virtue, every grace,
Ah! what avails the sceptred race.
Here you see the four of us,
And there are so many more of us,
Eldest sons that must succeed.
We know how Caesar conquered Gaul
And how to whack a cricket ball,
Apart from this our education
Lacks co-ordination.
Tho' we're young and tentative
And rather rip-representative
Scions of a noble breed,
We are the products of those homes serene and stately
Which only lately
Seem to have run to seed!

The Stately Homes of England
How beautiful they stand,
To prove the upper classes
Have still the upper hand;
Tho' the fact that they have to be rebuilt
And frequently mortgaged to the hilt
Is inclined to take the gilt
Off the gingerbread,
And certainly damps the fun
Of the eldest son.
But still we won't be beaten,
We'll scrimp and screw and save,
The playing-fields of Eton
Have made us frightfully brave,
And tho' if the Van Dycks have to go
And we pawn the Bechstein Grand,
We'll stand by the Stately Homes of England.

Here you see the pick of us,
You may be heartily sick of us
Still with sense we're all imbued.

We waste no time on vain regrets
And when we're forced to pay our debts
We're always able to dispose of
Rows and rows and rows of
Gainsboroughs and Lawrences,
Some sporting prints of Aunt Florence's,
Some of which are rather rude.
Altho' we sometimes flaunt our family conventions,
Our good intentions
Mustn't be misconstrued.

The Stately Homes of England
We proudly represent,
We only keep them up for
Americans to rent.
Tho' the pipes that supply the bathroom burst
And the lavatory makes you fear the worst,
It was used by Charles the First
Quite informally,
And later by George the Fourth
On a journey North.
The State Apartments keep their
Historical renown,
It's wiser not to sleep there
In case they tumble down;
But still if they ever catch on fire
Which, with any luck, they might,
We'll fight for the Stately Homes of England.

The Stately Homes of England,
Tho' rather in the lurch,
Provide a lot of chances
For psychical research.
There's the ghost of a crazy younger son
Who murdered in Thirteen Fifty One
An extremely rowdy nun
Who resented it,
And people who come to call
Meet her in the hall.
The baby in the guest wing
Who crouches by the grate,
Was walled up in the west wing

In Fourteen Twenty Eight.
If anyone spots the Queen of Scots
In a hand-embroidered shroud,
We're proud of the Stately Homes of England.

The Stately Homes of England
In valley, dale and glen
Produce a race of charming,
Innocuous young men.
Though our mental equipment may be slight
And we barely distinguish left from right
We are quite prepared to fight
For our principles,
Though none of us know so far
What they really are.
Our duty to the nation,
It's only fair to state,
Lies not in pro-creation
But what we pro-create;
And so we can cry
With kindling eye
As to married life we go,
What ho!
For the Stately Homes of England!

The Stately Homes of England,
Although a trifle bleak,
Historically speaking,
Are more or less unique,
We've a cousin who won the Golden Fleece
And a very peculiar fowling piece
Which was sent to Cromwell's niece,
Who detested it,
And rapidly sent it back
With a dirty crack.
A note we have from Chaucer
Contains a bawdy joke,
We also have a saucer
That Bloody Mary broke,
We've two pairs of tights
King Arthur's Knights
Had completely worn away,

Sing Hey!
For the Stately Homes of England!

THE VULTURE
Hilaire Belloc (LM)

The vulture eats between his meals
And that's the reason why
He very, very rarely feels
As well as you and I.

His eye is dull, his head is bald,
His neck is growing thinner.
Oh! what a lesson for us all
To only eat at dinner!

Programme 9

LIMERICK
Anon (HL)

There once was a person from Lyme
Who married three wives at a time.
When asked, 'Why a third?'
He replied, 'One's absurd,
And bigamy, sir, is a crime.'

SPINSTERS' SONG
Noël Coward (MM)

We're little Parish workers,
With indefinite desires,
Determined to improve the shining hour
Though years of firm repression
May have quenched our inward fires,
Undoubtedly we've turned a trifle sour.
We're busy little beavers,
And we decorate the Church.
Our moral standard's very, very high.
The flower of English manhood
May have left us in the lurch
But we know we'll go to Heaven when we die.

THE BUNNY POEM
Pam Ayres (LL)

I am a bunny rabbit
Sitting in my hutch
I like to sit up this end,
I don't care for that end much.
I'm glad tomorrow's Thursday
'Cause with a bit of luck,
As far as I remember
That's the day they pass the buck.

LIMERICK
Anon (LM)

A near-sighted fellow named Walter,
Led a glamorized lass to the altar;
A beauty he thought her,
Till some soap and water
Made her look like the Rock of Gibraltar.

MACAVITY: THE MYSTERY CAT
T. S. Eliot (LL)

Macavity's a Mystery Cat: he's called the Hidden Paw –
For he's the master criminal who can defy the Law.
He's the bafflement of Scotland Yard, the Flying Squad's
   despair:
For when they reach the scene of crime – *Macavity's not there!*

Macavity, Macavity, there's no one like Macavity,
He's broken every human law, he breaks the law of gravity.
His powers of levitation would make a fakir stare,
And when you reach the scene of crime – *Macavity's not
   there!*
You may seek him in the basement, you may look up in the
   air –
But I tell you once and once again, *Macavity's not there!*

Macavity's a ginger cat, he's very tall and thin;
You would know him if you saw him, for his eyes are
   sunken in.
His brow is deeply lined with thought, his head is highly
   domed;
His coat is dusty from neglect, his whiskers are uncombed.
He sways his head from side to side, with movements like a
   snake;
And when you think he's half asleep, he's always wide
   awake.

Macavity, Macavity, there's no one like Macavity,
For he's a fiend in feline shape, a monster of depravity.
You may meet him in a by-street, you may see him in the
   square –
But when a crime's discovered, then *Macavity's not there!*

He's outwardly respectable. (They say he cheats at cards.)
And his footprints are not found in any file of Scotland
   Yard's.
And when the larder's looted, or the jewel-case is rifled,
Or when the milk is missing, or another Peke's been stifled,
Or the greenhouse glass is broken, and the trellis past repair –
Ay, there's the wonder of the thing! *Macavity's not there!*

And when the Foreign Office find a Treaty's gone astray,
Or the Admiralty lose some plans and drawings by the way,
There may be a scrap of paper in the hall or on the stair –
But it's useless to investigate – *Macavity's not there!*
And when the loss has been disclosed, the Secret Service say:
'It *must* have been Macavity!' – but he's a mile away.
You'll be sure to find him resting, or a-licking of his thumbs,
Or engaged in doing complicated long division sums.

Macavity, Macavity, there's no one like Macavity,
There never was a Cat of such deceitfulness and suavity.
He always has an alibi, and one or two to spare:
At whatever time the deed took place – MACAVITY WASN'T
    THERE!
And they say that all the Cats whose wicked deeds are widely
    known
(I might mention Mungojerrie, I might mention
    Griddlebone)
Are nothing more than agents for the Cat who all the time
Just controls their operations: the Napoleon of Crime.

INDOOR GAMES NEAR NEWBURY
John Betjeman (LM)

In among the silver birches winding ways of tarmac wander
And the signs to Bussock Bottom, Tussock Wood and
    Windy Brake,
Gabled lodges, tile-hung churches, catch the lights of our
    Lagonda
As we drive to Wendy's party, lemon curd and Christmas
    cake.
Rich the makes of motor whirring,
Past the pine-plantation purring
Come up, Hupmobile, Delage!
Short the way your chauffeurs travel,
Crunching over private gravel
Each from out his warm garage.

Oh but Wendy, when the carpet yielded to my indoor
    pumps
There you stood, your gold hair streaming,
Handsome in the hall-light gleaming
There you looked and there you led me off into the game of
    clumps
Then the new Victrola playing
And your funny uncle saying
'Choose your partners for a fox-trot! Dance until it's *tea*
    o'clock!
'Come on, young 'uns, foot it featly!'
Was it chance that paired us neatly,
I, who loved you so completely,
You, who pressed me closely to you, hard against your party
    frock?

'Meet me when you've finished eating!' So we met and no
    one found us.
Oh that dark and furry cupboard while the rest played hide
    and seek!
Holding hands our two hearts beating in the bedroom silence
    round us,
Holding hands and hardly hearing sudden footsteps, thud and
    shriek.
Love that lay too deep for kissing –

'Where *is* Wendy? Wendy's missing!'
Love so pure it *had* to end,
Love so strong that *I* was frighten'd
When you gripped my fingers tight and
Hugging, whispered 'I'm your friend.'

Good-bye Wendy! Send the fairies, pinewood elf and larch
   tree gnome,
Spingle-spangled stars are peeping
At the lush Lagonda creeping
Down the winding ways of tarmac to the leaded lights of
   home.
There, among the silver birches,
All the bells of all the churches
Sounded in the bath-waste running out into the frosty air.
Wendy speeded my undressing,
Wendy is the sheet's caressing
Wendy bending gives a blessing,
Holds me as I drift to dreamland, safe inside my slumberwear.

YOU'RE THE TOP
Cole Porter (MM)

At words poetic, I'm so pathetic
That I always have found it best,
Instead of getting 'em off my chest,
To let 'em rest unexpressed.
I hate parading
My serenading,
As I'll probably miss a bar,
But if this ditty
Is not so pretty,
At least it'll tell you
How great you are.

You're the top!
You're the Colosseum.
You're the top!
You're the Louvre Museum.
You're a melody from a symphony by Strauss,
You're a Bendel bonnet,
A Shakespeare sonnet,
You're Mickey Mouse.
You're the Nile,
You're the Tow'r of Pisa,
You're the smile
On the Mona Lisa.
I'm a worthless check, a total wreck, a flop,
But if, baby, I'm the bottom
You're the top!

Your words poetic are not pathetic.
On the other hand, boy, you shine,
And I can feel after every line
A thrill divine
Down my spine.
Now gifted humans like Vincent Youmans
Might think that your song is bad,
But for a person who's just rehearsin'
Well, I gotta say this my lad:

You're the top!
You're Mahatma Gandhi.
You're the top!
You're Napoleon brandy.
You're the purple light of a summer night in Spain,
You're the National Gall'ry,
You're Garbo's sal'ry,
You're cellophane.
You're sublime,
You're a turkey dinner,
You're the time
Of the Derby winner.
I'm a toy balloon that is fated soon to pop,
But if, baby, I'm the bottom
You're the top!

You're the top!
You're a Ritz hot toddy.
You're the top!
You're a Brewster body.
You're the boats that glide on the sleepy Zuider Zee,
You're a Nathan panning,
You're Bishop Manning,
You're broccoli,
You're a prize,
You're a night at Coney,
You're the eyes
Of Irene Bordoni.
I'm a broken doll, a fol-de-rol, a blop,
But if, baby, I'm the bottom
You're the top!

You're the top!
You're an Arrow collar.
You're the top!
You're a Coolidge dollar.
You're the nimble tread of the feet of Fred Astaire,
You're an O'Neill drama,
You're Whistler's mama,
You're Camembert.
You're a rose,
You're Inferno's Dante,

You're the nose
On the great Durante.
I'm just in the way, as the French would say
'De trop,'
But if, baby, I'm the bottom
You're the top!

You're the top!
You're a Waldorf salad,
You're the top!
You're a Berlin ballad.
You're a baby grand of a lady and a gent,
You're an old Dutch master,
You're Mrs. Astor,
You're Pepsodent.
You're romance,
You're the steppes of Russia,
You're the pants on a Roxy usher.
I'm a lazy lout that's just about to stop,
But if, baby, I'm the bottom
You're the top!

You're the top!
You're a dance in Bali.
You're the top!
You're a hot tamale.
You're an angel, you, simply too, too, too diveen,
You're a Botticelli,
You're Keats,
You're Shelley,
You're Ovaltine.
You're a boon,
You're the dam at Boulder,
You're the moon over Mae West's shoulder.
I'm a nominee of the G.O.P. or GOP,
But if, baby, I'm the bottom
You're the top.

You're the top!
You're the Tower of Babel.
You're the top!
You're the Whitney Stable.

By the river Rhine,
You're a sturdy stein of beer,
You're a dress from Saks's,
You're next year's taxes,
You're stratosphere.
You're my thoist,
You're a Drumstick Lipstick,
You're da foist
In da Irish Svipstick.
I'm a frightened frog
That can find no log
To hop,
But if, baby, I'm the bottom
You're the top!

MARIA WHO MADE FACES AND A
DEPLORABLE MARRIAGE
Hilaire Belloc (HL)

Maria loved to pull a face:
And no such commonplace grimace
As you or I or anyone
Might make at grandmamma for fun.
But one where nose and mouth and all
Were screwed into a kind of ball,
The which – as you may well expect –
Produced a horrible effect
On those it was directed at.
One morning she was struck like that! –
Her features took their final mould
In shapes that made your blood run cold
And wholly lost their former charm.
Mamma, in agonised alarm,
Consulted a renowned Masseuse
 – An old and valued friend of hers –
Who rubbed the wretched child for days
In five and twenty different ways
And after that began again.
But all in vain! – But all in vain!
The years advance: Maria grows
Into a Blooming English Rose –
With every talent, every grace
(Save in this trifle of the face).
She sang, recited, laughed and played
At all that an accomplished maid
Should play with skill to be of note –
Golf, the Piano, and the Goat;
She talked in French till all was blue
And knew a little German too.
She told the tales that soldiers tell,
She also danced extremely well,
Her wit was pointed, loud and raw,
She shone at laying down the law,
She drank liqueurs instead of tea,
Her verse was admirably free
And quoted in the latest books –
But people couldn't stand her looks.

Her parents had with thoughtful care
Proclaimed her genius everywhere,
Nor quite concealed a wealth which sounds
Enormous – thirty million pounds –
And further whispered it that she
Could deal with it exclusively.
They did not hide her chief defect,
But what with birth and intellect
And breeding and such ample means,
And still in her delightful 'teens,
A girl like our Maria (they thought)
Should make the kind of match she ought.
Those who had seen her here at home
Might hesitate: but Paris? Rome? . . .
– The foreigners should take the bait.
And so they did. At any rate,
The greatest men of every land
Arrived in shoals to seek her hand,
Grand Dukes, Commanders of the Fleece,
Mysterious Millionaires from Greece,
And exiled Kings in large amounts,
Ambassadors and Papal Counts,
And Rastaquouères from Palamerez
And Famous Foreign Secretaries,
They came along in turns to call
But *all* – without exception, *all* –
Though with determination set,
Yet, when they actually *met*,
Would start convulsively as though
They had received a sudden blow,
And mumbling a discreet good-day
Would shuffle, turn and slink away.

The upshot of it was Maria
Was married to a neighbouring Squire
Who, being blind, could never guess
His wife's appalling ugliness.

LIMERICK
Anon (MM)

There was a young lady of Ryde
Who ate some green apples and died;
The apples fermented
Inside the lamented,
And made cider inside her inside.

Programme 10

I WONDER WHAT HAPPENED TO HIM
Noël Coward (HL)

The India that one read about
And may have been misled about
In one respect has kept itself intact.
Though 'Pukka Sahib' traditions may have cracked
And thinned
The good old Indian army's still a fact.
That famous monumental man
The Officer and Gentleman
Still lives and breathes and functions from Bombay to
    Katmandu.
At any moment one can glimpse
Matured or embryonic 'Blimps'
Vivaciously speculating as to what became of who.
Though Eastern sounds may fascinate your ear
When West meets West you're always sure to hear –

Whatever became of old Bagot?
I haven't seen him for a year.
Is it true that young Forbes had to marry that Faggot
He met in the Vale of Kashmir?
Have you had any news
Of that chap in the 'Blues',
Was it Prosser or Pyecroft or Pym?
He was stationed in Simla, or was it Bengal?
I know he got tight at a ball in Nepal
And wrote several four-letter words on the wall.
I wonder what happened to him!

Whatever became of old Shelley?
Is it true that young Briggs was cashiered
For riding quite nude on a push-bike through Delhi
The day the new Viceroy appeared?
Have you had any word
Of that bloke in the 'Third',

Was it Southerby, Sedgwick or Sim?
They had him thrown out of the club in Bombay
For, apart from his mess bills exceeding his pay,
He took to pig-sticking in *quite* the wrong way.
I wonder what happened to him!

One must admit that by and large
Upholders of the British Raj
Don't shine in conversation as a breed.
Though Indian army officers can read
A bit
Their verbal wit – has rather run to seed.
Their splendid insularity
And roguish jocularity
Was echoing through when Victoria was Queen.
In restaurants and dining-cars,
In messes, clubs and hotel bars
They try to maintain tradition in the way it's always been.
Though worlds may change and nations disappear
Above the shrieking chaos you will hear –

Whatever became of old Tucker?
Have you heard any word of young Mills
Who ruptured himself at the end of a chukka
And had to be sent to the hills?
They say that young Lees
Had a go of 'DTs'
And his hopes of promotion are slim.
According to Stubbs, who's a bit of a louse,
The silly young blighter went out on a 'souse',
And took two old tarts into Government House.
I wonder what happened to him!

Whatever became of old Keeling?
I hear that he got back from France
And frightened three nuns in a train in Darjeeling
By stripping and waving his lance!
D'you remember Munroe,
In the PAVO?
He was tallish and mentally dim.
That talk of heredity can't be quite true,
He was dropped on his head by his ayah at two,

I presume that by now he'll have reached GHQ.
I'm sure that's what happened to him!

Whatever became of old Archie?
I hear he departed this life
After rounding up ten sacred cows in Karachi
To welcome the Governor's wife.
D'you remember young Phipps
Who had *very* large hips
And whose waist was excessively slim?
Well, it seems that some doctor in Grosvenor Square
Gave him hormone injections for growing his hair
And he grew something here, and he grew something there.
I wonder what happened to her – him?

THE VILLAGE BURGLAR
Anon (LM)

Under the spreading gooseberry bush
The village burglar lies;
The burglar is a hairy man
With whiskers round his eyes.

He goes to church on Sundays;
He hears the Parson shout;
He puts a penny in the plate
And takes a shilling out.

THE JUMBLIES
Edward Lear (LL)

They went to sea in a Sieve, they did,
In a Sieve they went to sea:
In spite of all their friends could say,
On a winter's morn, on a stormy day,
In a Sieve they went to sea!
And when the Sieve turned round and round,
And every one cried, 'You'll all be drowned!'
They called aloud, 'Our Sieve ain't big,
But we don't care a button! we don't care a fig!
In a Sieve we'll go to sea!'
Far and few, far and few,
Are the lands where the Jumblies live;
Their heads are green, and their hands are blue,
And they went to sea in a Sieve.

They sailed in a Sieve, they did,
In a Sieve they sailed so fast,
With only a beautiful pea-green veil
Tied with a riband by way of a sail,
To a small tobacco-pipe mast;
And every one said, who saw them go,
'O won't they be soon upset, you know!
For the sky is dark, and the voyage is long,
And happen what may, it's extremely wrong
In a Sieve to sail so fast!'
Far and few, far and few,
Are the lands where the Jumblies live;
Their heads are green, and their hands are blue,
And they went to sea in a Sieve.

The water it soon came in, it did,
The water it soon came in;
So to keep them dry, they wrapped their feet
In a pinky paper all folded neat,
And they fastened it down with a pin.
And they passed the night in a crockery-jar,
And each of them said, 'How wise we are!
Though the sky be dark, and the voyage be long,
Yet we never can think we were rash or wrong,

While round in our Sieve we spin!'
Far and few, far and few,
Are the lands where the Jumblies live;
Their heads are green, and their hands are blue,
And they went to sea in a Sieve.

And all night long they sailed away;
And when the sun went down,
They whistled and warbled a moony song
To the echoing sound of a coppery gong,
In the shade of the mountains brown.
'O Timballo! How happy we are,
When we live in a sieve and a crockery-jar,
And all night long in the moonlight pale,
We sail away with a pea-green sail,
In the shade of the mountains brown!'
Far and few, far and few,
Are the lands where the Jumblies live;
Their heads are green, and their hands are blue,
And they went to sea in a Sieve.

They sailed to the Western Sea, they did,
To a land all covered with trees,
And they bought an Owl, and a useful Cart,
And a pound of Rice, and a Cranberry Tart,
And a hive of silvery Bees.
And they bought a Pig, and some green Jack-daws,
And a lovely Monkey with lollipop paws,
And forty bottles of Ring-Bo-Ree,
And no end of Stilton Cheese.
Far and few, far and few,
Are the lands where the Jumblies live;
Their heads are green, and their hands are blue,
And they went to sea in a Sieve.

And in twenty years they all came back,
In twenty years or more,
And every one said, 'How tall they've grown!
For they've been to the Lakes, and the Torrible Zone,
And the hills of the Chankly Bore;
And they drank their health, and gave them a feast
Of dumplings made of beautiful yeast;
And every one said, 'If we only live,
We too will go to sea in a Sieve, –
To the hills of the Chankly Bore!'
Far and few, far and few,
Are the lands where the Jumblies live;
Their heads are green, and their hands are blue,
And they went to sea in a Sieve.

LIMERICK
Langford Reed (MM)

A patriot living at Ewell
Found his bonfire wanted more fuel,
So he threw in Uncle James
To heighten the flames,
A measure effective though cruel.

POISONING THE PIGEONS IN THE PARK
Tom Lehrer (LM)

Spring is here, Spring is here,
Life is skittles and life is beer,
I think the loveliest time of the year
Is Spring. I do. Don't you? 'Course you do.

But there's one thing that makes Spring complete for me
And makes every Sunday a treat for me,
All the world seems in tune on a Spring afternoon,
When we're poisoning the pigeons in the park.

Every Sunday you'll see my sweetheart and me,
As we poison the pigeons in the park.
When they see us coming the birdies all try and hide
But they still go for peanuts when coated with cyanide.
The sun's shining bright, everything seems all right
When we're poisoning pigeons in the park.

We've gained notoriety and caused much anxiety
In the Audubon Society with our games.
They call it impiety and lack of propriety
And quite a variety of unpleasant names.
But it's not against any religion
To want to dispose of a pigeon
So if one day you are free why don't you come with me
And we'll poison the pigeons in the park.
And may be we'll do in a squirrel or two
While we're poisoning the pigeons in the park.

We'll murder them all 'mid laughter and merriment
Except for the few we take home to experiment.
My pulse will be quickening with each drop of strychnine
We feed to a pigeon – it takes just a smidgen,
To poison a pigeon in the park.

HAROLD THE FROG
Jeremy Lloyd (HL)

Harold a rather lonely frog,
With spotted, manly chest,
Lived in a wet and squelchy bog
And always looked depressed.
He couldn't get a froggy date,
Although he'd try each night
But when he'd squelch behind a girl
She'd just leap off in fright.
A wallflower at the local hop
He'd dance 'til dawn alone,
Quick, quick, quick, slow, quick
Plop, plop, plop.
Then squelch his way back home.
Reflecting in his private pool
On his unhappy fate,
He wondered why on earth it was
He couldn't get a date.
His friends all knew the reason why,
But friends don't like to tell
A frog who's got and doesn't know;
A wet and boggy smell!

BUSINESS GIRLS
John Betjeman (LM)

From the geyser ventilators
Autumn winds are blowing down
On a thousand business women
Having baths in Camden Town.

Waste pipes chuckle into runnels,
Stream's escaping here and there,
Morning trains through Camden cutting
Shake the Crescent and the Square.

Early nip of changeful autumn,
Dahlias glimpsed through garden doors,
At the back precarious bathrooms
Jutting out from upper floors;

And behind their frail partitions
Business women lie and soak,
Seeing through the draughty skylight
Flying clouds and railway smoke.

Rest you there, poor unbelov'd ones,
Lap your loneliness in heat.
All too soon the tiny breakfast,
Trolley-bus and windy street!

INCONSIDERATE HANNAH
Harry Graham (LL)

Naughty little Hannah said
She could make her Grandma whistle,
So, that night, inside her bed,
Placed some nettles and a thistle.

Though dear Grandma quite infirm is,
Heartless Hannah watched her settle,
With her poor old epidermis
Resting up against a nettle.

Suddenly she reached the thistle!
My! you should have heard her whistle!

A successful plan was Hannah's
But I cannot praise her manners.

WHO WANTS TO BE A MILLIONAIRE?
Cole Porter (MM)

Who has an itch
To be filthy rich?
Who gives a hoot
For a lot of loot?
Who longs to live
A life of perfect ease?
And be swamped by necessary luxuries?

Who wants to be a millionaire?
I don't.
Have flashy flunkies everywhere?
I don't.
Who wants the bother of a country estate?
A country estate
Is something I'd hate!
Who wants a fancy foreign car?
I don't.
Who wants to tire of caviar?
I don't.
Who wants a marble swimming pool too?
I don't.
And I don't,
'Cause all I want is you.

Who wants to be a millionaire?
I don't.
Who wants uranium to spare?
I don't.
Who wants to journey on a gigantic yacht?
Do I want a yacht?
Oh, how I do not!
Who wants to wallow in champagne?
I don't.
Who wants a supersonic plane?
I don't.
Who wants a private landing field too?
I don't.
And I don't,
'Cause all I want is you.

Who wants to be a millionaire?
I don't.
And go to ev'ry swell affair?
I don't.
Who wants to ride behind a liv'ried chauffeur?
A liv'ried chauffeur
Do I want? No, sir!
Who wants an op'ra box, I'll bet?
I don't.
And sleep through Wagner at the Met?
I don't.
Who wants to corner Cartier's too?
I don't.
And I don't.
'Cause all I want is you.

PEEKABOO, I ALMOST SEE YOU
Ogden Nash (LM)

Middle-aged life is merry, and I love to lead it,
But there comes a day when your eyes are all right but your
    arm isn't long enough to hold the telephone book where
    you can read it,
And your friends get jocular, so you go to the oculist,
And of all your friends he is the joculist,
So over his facetiousness let us skim,
Only noting that he has been waiting for you ever since you
    said Good evening to his grandfather clock under the
    impression that it was him,
And you look at his chart and it says SHRDLU QWERTYOP,
    and you say Well, why SHRDNTLU QWERTYOP? and he
    says one set of glasses won't do.
You need two,
One for reading Erle Stanley Gardner's Perry Mason and
    Keat's 'Endymion' with,
And the other for walking around without saying Hello to
    strange wymion with.
So you spend your time taking off your seeing glasses to put
    on your reading glasses, and then remembering that your
    reading glasses are upstairs or in the car,
And then you can't find your seeing glasses again because
    without them on you can't see where they are.
Enough of such mishaps, they would try the patience of an
    ox,
I prefer to forget both pairs of glasses and pass my declining
    years saluting strange women and grandfather clocks.

LIMERICK
Anon (MM)

A lisping young lady called Beth
Was saved from a fate worse than death
Seven times in a row,
Which unsettled her so,
That she stopped saying 'No' and said 'Yeth'.

Programme 11

STANDING ROOM ONLY
Spike Milligan (LM)

'This population explosion,'
Said Peter to St Paul,
'Is really getting far too much,
Just look at that crowd in the hall.
Even here in heaven
There isn't any room,
I think the world could do with less,
Much less fruit in the womb.'
Thus heaven is overcrowded,
The numbers are starting to tell,
So when the next lot knock at the gates,
Tell 'em to go to hell.

MATILDA WHO TOLD LIES, AND WAS
BURNED TO DEATH
Hilaire Belloc (MM)

Matilda told such Dreadful Lies,
It made one Gasp and Stretch one's Eyes;
Her Aunt, who, from her Earliest Youth,
Had kept a Strict Regard for Truth,
Attempted to Believe Matilda:
The effort very nearly killed her,
And would have done so, had not She
Discovered this Infirmity.
For once, towards the Close of Day,
Matilda, growing tired of play,
And finding she was left alone,
Went tiptoe to the Telephone
And summoned the Immediate Aid
Of London's Noble Fire-Brigade.
Within an hour the Gallant Band

Were pouring in on every hand,
From Putney, Hackney Downs, and Bow
With Courage high and Hearts a-glow
They galloped, roaring through the Town,
'Matilda's House is Burning Down!'
Inspired by British Cheers and Loud
Proceeding from the Frenzied Crowd,
They ran their ladders through a score
Of windows on the Ball Room Floor;
And took Peculiar Pains to Souse
The Pictures up and down the House,
Until Matilda's Aunt succeeded
In showing them they were not needed;
And even then she had to pay
To get the Men to go away!

It happened that a few Weeks later
Her Aunt was off to the Theatre
To see that Interesting Play
The Second Mrs Tanqueray.
She had refused to take her Niece
To hear this Entertaining Piece:
A Deprivation Just and Wise
To Punish her for Telling Lies.
That Night a Fire *did* break out —
You should have heard Matilda Shout!
You should have heard her Scream and Bawl,
And throw the window up and call
To People passing in the Street —
(The rapidly increasing Heat
Encouraging her to obtain
Their confidence) — but all in vain!
For every time She shouted 'Fire!'
They only answered 'Little Liar'!
And therefore when her Aunt returned,
Matilda, and the House, were Burned.

GEORGE THE GIRAFFE
Jeremy Lloyd (LL)

Young George the giraffe
Used to wear a big scarf
And in winter time donned a warm coat.
For he lived in a zoo
And had twice caught the flu,
And often he had a sore throat.
So far from his home
He'd stand there alone
And dream of the African plain,
Where he'd lived as a lad
With his mum and his dad
And he wished he could see them again.
For life in a zoo
When you're prone to the flu
And you've got the world's longest sore throat,
Despite thick pyjamas
And lots of bananas,
Makes you want to get on the next boat.
So next time you go to the zoo
And they show
Every animal there except one,
A lonely giraffe, in a coat and a scarf,
It means George has escaped to the sun.

LIMERICK
Anon (LM)

There was a young lady named Kent,
Who gave up her husband for Lent.
The night before Easter,
When Jesus released her,
It didn't make a damned bit of difference
because in the meantime he'd been running
around with a whole lot of other women.

THE POBBLE WHO HAS NO TOES
Edward Lear (HL)

The Pobble who has no toes
Had once as many as we;
When they said, 'Some day you may lose them all';
He replied – 'Fish Fiddle de-dee!'
And his Aunt Jobiska made him drink,
Lavender water tinged with pink,
For she said, 'The World in general knows
There's nothing so good for a Pobble's toes!'

The Pobble who has no toes,
Swam across the Bristol Channel;
But before he set out he wrapped his nose,
In a piece of scarlet flannel.
For his Aunt Jobiska said, 'No harm
Can come to his toes if his nose is warm;
And it's perfectly known that a Pobble's toes
Are safe – provided he minds his nose.'

The Pobble swam fast and well,
And when boats or ships came near him
He tinkledy-binkledy-winkled a bell,
So that all the world could hear him.
And all the Sailors and Admirals cried,
When they saw him nearing the further side,
'He has gone to fish, for his Aunt Jobiska's
Runcible Cat with crimson whiskers!'

But before he touched the shore,
The shore of the Bristol Channel,
A sea-green Porpoise carried away
His wrapper of scarlet flannel.
And when he came to observe his feet,
Formerly garnished with toes so neat,
His face at once became forlorn
On perceiving that all his toes were gone!

And nobody ever knew
From that dark day to the present,
Whoso had taken the Pobble's toes,

In a manner so far from pleasant.
Whether the shrimps or crawfish gray,
Or crafty Mermaids stole them away –
Nobody knew; and nobody knows
How the Pobble was robbed of his twice five toes!

The Pobble who has no toes
Was placed in a friendly Bark,
And they rowed him back, and carried him up,
To his Aunt Jobiska's Park.
And she made him a feast at his earnest wish
Of eggs and buttercups fried with fish;
And she said, 'It's a fact the whole world knows,
That Pobbles are happier without their toes.'

HOME. 99 44/100% SWEET HOME
Ogden Nash (LM)

Most of the time, oh most of the time,
I like to sit at home,
With a good fire, and a good chair,
And a good detective tome.
What can a man, can a family man
Ask in the way of cheer
More than a pipe, and a reading lamp,
And a modest mug of beer?
Most of the time, the wealth of the Indies
Wouldn't tempt me to blowouts or shindies.

But once in a while,
Oh, once in a while,
It's pleasant to paint the town,
To frolic and revel,
A regular devil,
And do the evening brown.
To buy an orchid, or maybe two,
And woo the way that you used to woo,
To press the loot from the babies' banks
On waiters who fail to murmur thanks,
To dine and wine and dance and sup,
And ride in a cab till the sun comes up,
And to feel thereafter, in sundry ways,
Simply awful for days and days.
Home is heaven and orgies are vile,
But I *like* an orgy, once in a while.

Home is the place, oh home is the place
That no place else is like,
So who would freeze in the South, like Byrd,
Or discover peaks, like Pike?
Who so animal, who so low
As to pant for the Great White Way?
Who would give up a night at home
For one in a cabaret?
Most of the time I'd swim to Australia
As soon as engage in a Saturnalia.

But once in a while,
Oh, once in a while,
It's pleasant to loop the loop,
To daringly seize
The flying trapeze
With a cry of Allez-oop!
To jump the rails, kick over the traces,
To go on the town and visit places,
Sit ten at a table meant for two,
And choke on smoke as you used to do.
To tread the floor with the dancing bears,
They on your feet, and you on theirs,
To have flings at things that philosophers true shun,
And undermine your constitue-shun.
Home is heaven and orgies are vile,
But you *need* an orgy, once in a while.

SARDINES
Spike Milligan (MM)

A baby Sardine
Saw her first submarine:
She was scared and watched through a peephole.

'Oh, come, come, come,'
Said the Sardine's mum,
'It's only a tin full of people.'

UNCLE HARRY
Noël Coward (HL)

We all of us have relations
Our crosses in life we bear,
A gloomy group of uncles, cousins and aunts,
We meet them in railway stations,
In Harrods or Chester Square,
And always on the Channel boat to France.
We have to be polite to them,
They sometimes send us pheasants,
We always have to write to them,
To thank for Christmas presents.
These family obligations
Admittedly are a bore
But I possess one uncle that I positively adore.

Poor Uncle Harry
Wanted to be a missionary
So he took a ship and sailed away.
This visionary,
Hotly pursued by dear Aunt Mary,
Found a South Sea Isle on which to stay.
The natives greeted them kindly and invited them to dine
On yams and clams and human hams and vintage coconut
    wine,
The taste of which was filthy but the after-effects divine.
Poor Uncle Harry
Got a bit gay and longed to tarry.
This, Aunt Mary couldn't quite allow,
She lectured him severely on a number of church affairs
But when she'd gone to bed he made a get-away down the
    stairs,
For he longed to find the answer to a few of the maiden's
    prayers.
Uncle Harry's not a missionary now.

Poor Uncle Harry
After a chat with dear Aunt Mary
Thought the time had come to make a row,
He lined up all the older girls in one of the local sheds
And while he was reviling them and tearing them to shreds

They took their Mother Hubbards off and tied them round
  their heads.
Uncle Harry's not a missionary now.
He's awfully happy
But he's certainly not a missionary now!

Now Uncle was just a 'seeker',
A 'dreamer' sincerely blest,
Of this there couldn't be a shadow of doubt.
The fact that his flesh was weaker
Than even Aunt Mary guessed
Took even her some time to figure out.
In all those languid latitudes
The atmosphere's exotic,
To take up moral attitudes
Would be too idiotic,
Though nobody could be meeker
Than Uncle had been before
I bet today he's giving way
At practically every pore!

Poor Uncle Harry
Having become a missionary
Found the natives' morals rather crude.
He and Aunt Mary
Quickly imposed an arbitrary
Ban on them shopping in the nude.
They all considered this silly and they didn't take it well,
They burnt his boots and several suits and wrecked the
  Mission Hotel,
They also burnt his mackintosh, which made a disgusting
  smell.
Poor Uncle Harry
After some words with dear Aunt Mary
Called upon the chiefs for a pow-wow.
They didn't brandish knives at him, they really were awfully
  sweet,
They made concerted dives at him and offered him things to
  eat,
But when they threw their wives at him he had to admit
  defeat.
Uncle Harry's not a missionary now.

Poor dear Aunt Mary
Though it were revolutionary
Thought *her* time had come to take a bow.
Poor Uncle Harry looked at her, in whom he had placed his
    trust,
His very last illusion broke and crumbled away to dust
For she'd placed a flower behind her ear and frankly exposed
    her bust.
Uncle Harry's not a missionary now.
He's left the island
But he's certainly not a missionary now.

LIMERICK
Ogden Nash (LM)

There was a brave girl of Connecticut
Who flagged the express with her pecticut;
Which her elders defined
As presence of mind,
But deplorable absence of ecticut.

TO MAKE A WHALE
Pam Ayres (LL)

Man is gloriously clever
Making intricate machines
And complicated gadgetry
And bigger runner beans
And journeys into space
With mighty rockets in the tail -
But when the last one's towed away
He couldn't make

a whale.

LET'S MISBEHAVE
Cole Porter (MM)

You could have a great career,
And you should.
Only one thing stops you, dear,
You're too good.
If you want a future, darling,
Why don't you get a past?
'Cause that fatal moment's coming,
At last.

We're all alone
No chaperon
Can get our number,
The world's in slumber,
Let's misbehave.
There's something wild
About you, child,
That's so contagious,
Let's be outrageous,
Let's misbehave.
When Adam won Eve's hand,
He wouldn't stand for teasin',
He didn't care about
Those apples out of season.
They say that spring
Means just one thing
To little love birds
We're not above birds,
Let's misbehave.

It's getting late
And while I wait
My poor heart aches on,
Why keep the brakes on?
Let's misbehave.
I feel quite sure.
Un peu d'amour
Would be attractive,
While we're still active,
Let's misbehave.

You know my heart is true,
And you say, you for me care;
Somebody's sure to tell,
But what the hell do we care?
They say that bears
Have love affairs,
And even camels;
We're merely mammals,
Let's misbehave.

INDEX OF AUTHORS

INDEX OF FIRST LINES

INDEX OF TITLES

ACKNOWLEDGEMENTS

For permission to reprint copyright material, the publishers gratefully acknowledge the following:

Maya Angelou: 'Come And Be My Baby' reprinted by permission of Virago Press. Pam Ayres: 'I'm The Dog Who Didn't Win A Prize', 'The Horse's Farewell To His Cowboy', 'The Bunny Poem' and 'To Make A Whale' from *The Works* © Pam Ayres 1992. Hilaire Belloc: 'Jim . . .', 'Henry King . . .', 'Charles Augustus Fortescue . . .', 'Lord Finchley', 'Rebecca . . .', 'Maria . . .', 'Matilda . . .', 'Fatigue', 'The Vulture' from *Cautionary Verses*, Random House, reprinted by permission of the Peters Fraser & Dunlop Group Ltd. John Betjeman: 'Slough', 'Executive', 'In A Bath Teashop', 'A Subaltern's Love-Song', 'Indoor Games Near Newbury', 'Business Girls' reprinted by permission of John Murray (Publishers) Ltd. Charles Causley: 'I Saw A Jolly Hunter' from *Collected Poems*, Macmillan, reprinted by permission of David Higham Associates. G. K. Chesterton: 'Rolling English Road', 'The Song Of The Quoodle' reprinted by permission of A. P. Watt Ltd on behalf of The Royal Literary Fund. Wendy Cope: 'Loss', 'English Weather' from *Serious Concerns*, 'Prelude' from *Making Cocoa For Kingsley Amis*, reprinted by permission of Faber and Faber. Noël Coward: 'A Bar On The Piccola Marina', 'Mrs Worthington', 'Mad Dogs And Englishmen', 'Choir Boys' Song', 'Alice Is At It Again', 'Let's Do It', 'I've Been To A Marvellous Party', 'The Stately Homes Of England', 'Spinsters' Song', 'I Wonder What Happened To Him', 'Uncle Harry' reprinted by permission of Michael Imison Playwrights Ltd on behalf of the Noël Coward Estate. Roald Dahl: 'A Little Nut Tree', 'A Hand In The Bird', 'Mary Mary' from *Rhyme Stew*, Jonathan Cape and Penguin Books. George Marriott Edgar: 'The Lion and Albert', words by George Marriott Edgar © 1933, reproduced by permission of Francis Day and Hunter Ltd. T. S. Eliot: 'Macavity The Mystery Cat', 'Mungojerrie And Rumpelteazer' from *Old Possum's Book Of Practical Cats*, reprinted by permission of Faber and Faber. Joyce Grenfell: 'Stately As A Galleon' © Joyce Grenfell 1978. Christopher Isherwood: 'The Common Cormorant' reprinted by permission of Curtis Brown on behalf of the Executors of the Estate of Christopher Isherwood, copyright © Christopher Isherwood, 1966. Tom Lehrer: 'Be Prepared', 'When You Are Old And Gray', 'Poisoning Pigeons In The Park', reprinted by permission of Tom Lehrer. Jeremy Lloyd; 'A Penniless French Mouse', 'My Best Friend', 'Harold The Frog', 'George The Giraffe', reprinted by permission of Alexandra Cann. Roger McGough: 'Discretion' from *Watchwords*, Jonathan Cape, reprinted by permission of the Peters Fraser & Dunlop Group Ltd. Edna St. Vincent Millay: 'First Fig' from *Collected Poems*, HarperCollins. Copyright 1922, 1950 by Edna St. Vincent Millay, reprinted by permission of Elizabeth Barnett, literary executor. Spike Milligan: 'English Teeth', 'The Pig', 'Love Conquers', 'Standing Room Only', 'Sardines' reprinted by permission of Spike Milligan Productions Ltd. Adrian Mitchell: 'Celia, Celia' from *For Beauty Douglas*, Allison & Busby, reprinted by permission of the Peters Fraser & Dunlop Group Ltd. Jan Morris: 'Pig Rhyme' reprinted by permission of A. P. Watt Ltd on behalf of Jan Morris. Ogden Nash: 'There Was An Old Man In A Trunk' copyright © 1934 by Ogden Nash,

OTHER BOXTREE TITLES

0 7522 0500 5	Animal Lovers	£5.99 pb
0 7522 0678 8	Baldyman: Creating an Impression	£7.99 pb
0 7522 0943 4	Beavis and Butthead: This Book Sucks	£6.99 pb
0 7522 0854 3	Always Postpone Meetings With Time Wasting Morons	£4.99 pb
0 7522 0136 0	Bring Me The Head of Willy The Mail Boy	£4.99 pb
0 7522 0849 7	Shave The Whales	£4.99 pb
0 7522 0179 4	Ellen	£7.99 pb
0 7522 0632 X	Eurotrash: A Weird Guide to Europe	£10.99 pb
0 7522 0832 2	Fleas, Knees and Hidden Elephants	£4.99 hb
0 7522 0615 X	Foxtrot	£4.99 pb
0 7522 0620 6	Foxtrot: Pass the Loot	£4.99 pb
0 7522 0184 0	Friends	£9.99 pb
0 7522 0745 8	Get Lucky: Diary of Lord Lucan	£9.99 hb
0 7522 0896 9	Gordon Brittas: Sharing the Dream	£6.99 pb

Boxtree Cash Sales, P.O. Box 11, Falmouth, Cornwall TR10 9EN

Please send a cheque or postal order for the value of the book and add the following for postage and packing:

U.K. including B.F.P.O. – £1.00 for one book plus 50p for the second book, and 30p for each additional book ordered up to a £3.00 maximum.

Overseas including Eire – £2.00 for the first book plus £1.00 for the second book, and 50p for each additional book ordered.

OR please debit this amount from my Access/Visa Card (delete as appropriate).

Card Number ☐☐☐☐☐☐☐☐☐☐☐☐☐☐☐☐

Amount £ ....

Expiry Date ....

Signed ....

Name ....

Address ....